MOMENTS OF GRATITUDE

GIVING GOD THANKS FOR THE "LITTLE" BLESSINGS

Janice Hylton Thompson

Unless otherwise indicated, all scriptures are taken from the King James Version and the New King James Version.

Copyright © 1982 by Thomas Nelson, Inc.
Used by permission. All rights reserved."

{Please note that scriptures in book are highlighted for effect.}

Copyright © 2020
by Janice Hylton-Thompson
All rights reserved.

Cover Designed by Rebecca Covers

Edited by Wordwors1

Interior Format by Richa Bargotrar

ISBN: 978-1-946242-12-9

Janice Hylton Thompson
P. O. Box 422
Bellville NJ 07109

No part of this book may be reproduced in any form without the written permission of the author, except for brief passages included in a review. However, written permission not needed when quotations are used in church bulletins, orders of service, Sunday school lessons, church newsletters and similar works in the course of Christian instruction or services at a place of Christian worship or other Christian assembly.

Table of Contents

Thank You, Lord 1
Dedication 3
Personal Note 5
Personal Note of Feelings 7
Moments of Gratitude 9
A Moment in Time 11
How Moments of Gratitude Came About 13
Moments of Gratitude 16
Journal 21
Testimony Time and New Dating Journal 161
Final Words 165
Few of my Go-to and Favorite Psalms 167
About the Author 184

Thank You, Lord

When I think about the goodness of the Lord and all that he has done for me, my very soul cries out, *"Hallelujah, hallelujah,*
THANK YOU, GOD, FOR SAVING ME!!"

All glory, honor, praise, power, worship, and majesty be unto the Lord! Lord, I am so thankful for you keeping Alexia and me! You blessed and provided for us, and you made a way out for us.

Lord, I count our blessings, and I name them one by one. Thank you, Lord!! I am reminded of a song I used to sing as a little girl in Sunday school in our hut in Jamaica.

It goes, *"Birds in the treetop praising the Lord, flowers in the garden bowing down their heads, trees waving their branches, then why shouldn't I, why shouldn't I praise the Lord?*

Thank you, Lord

Dedication

To my sweet and dearest Alexia, aka Lexi. I am remembering you being about three years old as I type this. I was kneeling at my bed in our little studio apartment. I was praying and crying out to the Lord for everything that was going on in our lives.

You came over and rubbed my leg and said, "Mommy, don't cry. It's going to be ok."

Oh, that made me want to weep like a baby, and weep, I did. And whenever I faced challenging times over the last almost 30 years, I remembered that moment when you, my little Lexi, said, "Mommy, don't cry, it's going to be ok."

And so, to my sweet Lexi, I say, *"Thank You, and I love you very much. I could not have been where I am today if it wasn't for you. You have been such a blessing to me, and you have caused me to be stronger in my walk and faith in the Lord Jesus. Thank you, my love.*

Affectionately, Mom

Personal Note

Hello, my beloved reader,

When I reviewed my journals for publishing Moments of Gratitude book, reading many of these entries brought many emotions back to my memory this Thanksgiving season.

However, I noticed the main thing was how the prayers I prayed, the confessions I made, the tithes and offerings that I gave, and the words I spoke over mine and Alexia's lives came to fruition.

So, as you read and wait for your breakthrough, I want you to keep in mind my testimony. Every time I prayed for my husband, he began to manifest himself, slowly but surely.

And at the publication of Moments of Gratitude, we have been happily married for almost eight years. Ladies, my husband is the man I have prayed for, for years.

The Lord has blessed and prospered Lexi and me. I am so grateful, and I thank the Lord daily. May the Lord shower you with blessings and manifestations of the prayers you prayed.

Blessings Always
Janice

Personal Note of Feelings

Hello, my beloved reader,

You know, as I read over Moments of Gratitude, one last time before I send it off to the formatter, I cannot help but feel so vulnerable and naked.

Moments of Gratitude, journal entries are some of the lowest moments in my walk and faith in our Lord and Savior Jesus Christ.

But, when I look at my life now and where God has brought Lexi and me from and to, I am at peace.

And it brings great joy and a smile to my face to share these vulnerable moments with you. Because I know, like me, you might be going through a rough time right now.

Be assured, my beloved, that as the Lord brought me through, he will do the same with you. I absolutely love and adore you.

Love You

Janice

Moments of Gratitude

Moments of Gratitude is for every brother or sister in Christ, going through a rough time. I have lived long enough to know that life happens. Often, we get discouraged and even depressed because things are not going the way we had hoped.

One of the hardest things for me to deal with over the last twenty-six years is that I have a child with special needs. But, with God's grace and mercy, the Lord gave me enough strength to get up and get my baby girl the help she needed.

Regardless of what is going on in your life, I encourage you to hang in there! Our Heavenly Father promised us that He would never leave or forsake us and that He is with us always.

As you read *Moments of Gratitude*, I encourage you to take a moment and look for those *little* things that God is doing in your life and say, "*Thank You, Lord.*" You may think there isn't anything to be thankful for, but I guarantee you that there is. Look at the sunshine, the flowers, and the birds singing in the trees. Look in the eyes of your children, which I believe are the gateway of looking into the eyes of the Lord.

Today, and every day, know that you are not alone. I am reminded of the scripture that talks about a cloud of witnesses in Hebrews 12. As we read the stories of testimonies, trials, and tribulations of our forefathers and foremothers, we gain insight into their faith.

Therefore, their stories will strengthen us so that we can begin to dig our way out of our pits of sadness, depression, and discouragement. Every day start your day with a little bit of thanksgiving. If you feel there is nothing to be thankful for when you wake up, I encourage you to look for your *moments of gratitude*.

Let me be clear if you are depressed, and you know you need to seek professional help. I encourage you to do so. For years, the church has ignorantly taught that mental illness is demonic. We know now that many people have chemical imbalances in their brains, and medication is needed. Please call a doctor, talk to a professional counselor, or tell someone. Most importantly, if you feel as if you might hurt yourself or anyone else, please call 911.

As I review this book for publication, I had to call the police to do a welfare check on someone who said they felt like hurting themselves. If you feel like hurting yourself, please tell someone, and my prayer is that they will call 911 for you. Please do not be ashamed. Living is essential, and you are loved and needed.

My philosophy is to pray but seek medical help in the meantime. Be blessed, and I pray that you are blessed by my *Moments of Gratitude*. I love you with the Love of the Lord. Let's do this together.

A Moment in Time

Moment: A moment is a period that can be a second, minute, or an hour. *Moments* are also a day, month, season, year, or even a lifetime. Our experiences are comprised of moments. They can be good or bad, joyous or sad, encouraging or depressing, hurtful or healing.

We all have MOMENTS that can either build or destroy us. God designs some to bless and encourage us. Others are designed for pruning, disciplining. In the meantime, some *moments* help us to grow in our faith and walk with the Lord. Some *moments* we take with us for a lifetime, while others should be left as they are.

If you're not careful, you can get stuck in some moments, which can destroy your hopes, dreams, desires, and wishes. Additionally, the enemy designs some *moments* because he plans to kill, steal, and destroy. Differentiating between *moments* is imperative for your growth and survival.

Therefore, during every trial, test, and tribulation, an attitude of praise and thanksgiving is necessary.

Finally, always remember that God, our father, still sits on the throne and deserves all glory, honor, and adoration despite our circumstances.

How Moments of Gratitude Came About

For years, I've kept a journal of the things that God is doing in my life. I call it *"My Thank You Journal."* Some entries are thanksgiving. I share my heart in others, while a few are about disappointments and discouragements. No matter what it was, how big or small, I write it down in my journal and go back and read it every so often.

For *Moments of Gratitude*, I decided to add another journal that I had about my time with the Lord in prayer, seeking His face and hearing from Him. Reading it over brings me so much joy, peace, and contentment, especially since, fifteen and twenty years later, I can see the manifestation of those prayers I prayed.

I never thought that my journal would turn into a book. But isn't that how God works sometimes? The experiences He uses to either bless or teach us, He often encourages us to share as a testimony to help others.

Like any other believer, I have had many disappointments and sad times in my life and walk with the Lord. There were discouraging times and situations. My prayers' answers didn't always manifest when I wanted them to, which was difficult. I stood in some instances, and sometimes, I fell in my faith.

Despite all this, I have never wanted to turn my back on God and bow my knees to any other 'god.' I learned incredibly early that there is only one true and living God. And that Jesus Christ is the Son of God, who gave His life for me. Because of some of the things I was going through, my fellowship with the Lord might have been affected.

I wasn't praying, fasting, reading my Bible, praising, and worshipping Him as I did in the "good days."

While my fellowshipping varied, my relationship with the Lord remained the same. Nothing I did could change God's love for me as his child. Because a relationship with God is who we are to him.

Moments of Gratitude

One day, as I arrived at the dollar store, a car pulled out of a parking space ahead of me. I was happy and thankful because I just needed to run into the store and get one thing. However, when the gentleman looked behind him and saw that I was waiting to park, he stepped on his brakes and backed back into the parking space.

I got upset because the space was right in front of the store, and it would have been perfect for me. I drove down about half a block, and there was a parking space available. I got out to put money in the meter and noticed there were ten minutes on it already! I smiled, shook my head, and said, *"Thank you, Lord!"*

The Lord said in return, MOMENTS OF GRATITUDE. The exciting thing about these *moments* is that they can happen at any time. But sometimes, you must look for them.

You see, the Lord knows more than we do. He has a plan for us, but if we're not in tune with Him, we can have a different plan for our lives. He sees the future, and we don't. While I was busy getting upset at the man for backing back into the parking space, the Lord already had a parking space for me where I wouldn't have to put any money in the meter.

And then I began to think about all those times that I was writing about the things God was doing. God had a plan because half this book is filled with the blessings I wrote down in times of testing, trials, and tribulations. I was writing down what I call the *little* things God was doing.

Also, God knew that I would face tough times in my life, and it would be those little *"thank you" moments* I wrote down that would help me get through those times of hopelessness. On those days when I felt I had nothing to be thankful for, I needed to give thanks to the Lord, even if it meant looking for things to be grateful for.

In addition to the *Moments of Gratitude* book, I have also written the *Moments of Gratitude Thank You Journal*. So, as you read, I encourage you to write down your *moments of gratitude* in your journal. David said in **Psalm 103:1-2, "Bless the Lord, O my soul: and all that is within me, bless His holy name. Bless the Lord, O my soul, and forget not all His benefits."**

Writing down those little things that God is doing will help you not forget His benefits. Often, we look for *BIG* blessings: the house, car, mate, and or children. But, in the meantime, God is doing *little* things that we don't take time to be thankful for.

For example, you arrived at work safely. Did you say, "Thank you, Lord"? While you were at work, it started to rain, but you didn't have an umbrella to keep you dry as you walk to your car. You whisper a little prayer, "Lord, I pray it to stop raining before I get off work."

Just as you're about to get off work, it stopped raining. Did you say thank you? Did you even remember that you whispered that little prayer? Those are a few of the little things we may overlook. However, what would happen to us if we began to *look* for those little things God is doing and thank Him for them?

Now, I know that some things will happen in our lives that break and discourage us. For example, I cannot imagine the pain of losing a child. I have been blessed with two beautiful and healthy children, and every day I look at them and thank God.

My beloveth, no matter what you are going through, remember always that there is a God who sits high and looks low. I know some people who have walked away from God because He didn't show up during a situation or didn't stop an attack or a crime. And they asked the question, "Where was God, and why didn't He stop it?" I have learned that some answers we will never get here on earth.

The following are a few of my daily *'Moments of Gratitude'* and prayers that I prayed. I am sharing them to help you in your valleys or pits of despair. I encourage you to write your own *'Moments of Gratitude'* in the *Moments of Gratitude Thank You Journal*, and watch God bring you out of your pit of despair or wilderness experience.

The fantastic thing about my *moments of gratitude* is that some of these blessings happened ten or fifteen years ago. As I transcribed my *moments of gratitude* from my journals to my computer, I had to stop and think back about the goodness of the Lord.

Sometimes, when we feel down, depressed, angry, or bitter, if we can begin to say, *"Thank you Lord for waking me up this morning,"* it will help us to feel better, and the Holy Spirit will manifest Himself.

Remember, God is working in our lives every day and blessing us. We need to take time to recognize His blessings and give thanks for them. Another idea is this - if you can take one scripture per day and meditate on it and continually give God thanks for it, then you can dig your way out of your pit of despair.

The rest of this book has some of my *'Moments of Gratitude'* that began as a *Thank You Journal*, where I kept a record of the things God was doing in my life. Many of them are not what I would call *"big"* things, but they are everyday things that God was doing.

I pray that you will be blessed and encouraged by my entries and that you will begin to keep a record of all the beautiful things that God is doing in your life, ministry, and the lives of your loved ones. Remember, sometimes you will need to search for the *'little'* things God is so graciously doing in your life.

April 12, 2003 — You

Father, I thank you for "YOU." I am thankful for the Godhead, Father, Son, the manifestation of Jesus Christ, and the Holy Ghost. Thank you for your goodness, guidance, protection, and tender mercies.

Thank you, Lord, for blessing us with the Holy Spirit, who teaches us and bring your word to our remembrance. Thank you, Father, for Jesus Christ, who died for the sins of the world. Thank you, Lord.

Father, I thank you for the love of my life, my daughter Alexia. Lord, I thank you for Alexia. I love her with all my heart. She is very special to me, and she makes me very proud and happy to be her mom.

Thank you for trusting me with her. She is anointed, called, and chosen for a time like this.

Thank you, Lord, that she will continue to love you with all her heart, mind, soul, and body. She will proclaim the Word of the Lord, and she will walk in your ways and word, always.

June 1, 2003 — Prayer of Jabez

God the Father, God the Son, and God the Holy Spirit. By the leading of the Holy Spirit, Abba Father led me to read *"The Prayer of Jabez for Women"* by Bruce Wilkinson.

Truly, it has been a blessing to me. Doors began to open, blessings began to come in, and I am so thankful to you for that.

June 10, 2003 — Declare and Decree

Father, Holy Spirit, in the name of Jesus, I pray that:

1. I will rely on you, that my heart will be perfected towards you and that you will show yourself strong for me. I am reminded of the scripture in **2 Chronicles 16:8 Were not the Ethiopians and the Lubims a huge host, with very many chariots and horsemen? yet, because thou didst rely on the Lord, he delivered them into thine hand.**
2. I will strengthen myself against my enemies, and I will walk in the ways of the Lord always.
3. I pray that we will prepare our hearts to see you.

June 27, 2003 — Give, and It Shall Be Given to You

Thank you, Lord, for leading me to sow a seed of $100 in Pastor Bradshaw's life, my father in the gospel. I asked him to believe with me to increase my ministry, job, family, car, etc.

July 1, 2003 — My Jabez Moment

Reading the *"Prayer of Jabez"* and looking for my Jabez moment. I received a call about a job position I had applied for about three or four months ago. However, I wasn't qualified for it, and they hired someone else.

Father, I might not be qualified by man's standard but thank you, Lord, that you have qualified me.

Thankfully, even though I don't have a social worker degree, because I have a B.S in Psychology, the employer said they could hire me for a different position with my degree. The position pays about $30k per year, but I believe in you for the increase. Hours are 10:30 a.m.-7:30 p.m. due to the evening program.

At first, I wasn't going to take the position due to Alexia's schooling, but I thank God that you led me to an After-School Program that gets out at 7 p.m. Nevertheless, Lord, I believe that my hours will be 10:30 to 6:30. So, I believe in you for my Jabez moment.

July 7, 2003 — It Was God's Grace

I got off work and drove down Rt 280 to get home. There was an SUV that had flipped over. I stopped, got out of my car, and began to pray in the spirit. I also called a few people and asked them to pray. The woman came out of the SUV without being hurt or scratched up. I got a second to say to her that it was God's grace and mercy that kept her. Thank you, Lord.

July 10, 2003 — Free Checks

I went to my bank to order some checks, and I wanted to have the word of the Lord on them because, in everything I do, I want you, Lord, to receive all the glory and honor. My order came to over $40.

As I went back to my car, I decided to go back inside and ask the clerk about the checks' designs. Not only were the designs the same, but he also informed me that there was no cost for the checks because I had ordered them before. Therefore, the checks were free. Thank you, Lord, for blessing me with free checks.

July 11, 2003 — How Many Babies?

While at work on my Motor Meals activity at Saint Barnabas Hospital, a pregnant woman walked towards me in the lobby. I thought to myself, "Gosh, there must be about 3 or 4 babies in there." So, I asked her, and she said there were three babies in there.

Wow!! She asked that I say a prayer for her as she called her family. I waited for her to finish her call and then asked if I could pray for her right there. She said yes. She seemed nervous and afraid, and she was trembling. Right there in the lobby, I prayed for her that everything would work out, and I hoped to see her and her babies again. Thank you, Lord, for using me.

July 12, 2003 — Write the Vision

Spirit of the living God, father in the name of Jesus Christ, I just want to say thank you, Lord. I want to take the time to make a record of your goodness to Alexia and me, our family, because, Lord, truly, you have been good to us.

July 31, 2003 — Take Authority

For the past 2-3 weeks, Lord, you have been taking me through a breakage. Thank you for breaking things off and out of me. I had to let some friendships and people go. I have hurt like never. But Lord, I thank you because, finally, I am in a place where I can wait for you for the blessings you have for me. Thank you for manifesting your patience in me.

I felt as if I was oppressed in my mind by the devil. You spoke to me, *"Take Authority."* Lord, thank you because, as I began to take authority and talk about the word of the Lord and as I played the *song "Arise in Me and Demonstrate Your Power,"* a breakthrough began to take place.

When I woke up, I could sense that there was a change in my life. You broke something off me because the anointing destroys yokes, and burdens were lifted. Thank you, Lord. You said I should give it all to you and you will take care of it. So, Lord, I give it all to you now in Jesus' name.

July 31, 2003 Avenge Me of Mine Adversaries

Lord, thank you for avenging me of my adversaries. I dozed off around 5:30 a.m., and you spoke a word in my spirit. When I woke up, I could hear it repeatedly playing in my spirit. **Psalm 24:1 The earth is the Lord and the fulness thereof; the world and they that dwell therein.**

August 3, 2003   I Will Repay

Today, I woke up with "I will repay" in my spirit. Lord, you reminded me of the Amalekites in **1 Samuel 15:2-3 Thus saith the Lord of hosts, I remember that which Amalek did to Israel, how he laid wait for him in the way, when he came up from Egypt.**

³ Now go and smite Amalek, and utterly destroy all that they have, and spare them not; but slay both man and woman, infant and suckling, ox and sheep, camel and ass.

Also, you reminded me of **Philippians 4:6 Be careful for nothing; but in every thing by prayer and supplication with thanksgiving let your requests be made known unto God.** Father, I thank you for those words of encouragement. God, you are not in any haste to do anything.

You are not impatient as we are, but you're the God of heaven and earth. You are the beginning and the end, Alpha and Omega. You know it all. You're full of grace and mercy. So, Lord, as you told me a few weeks ago, *"Give it all to me, and I'll take care of it."* Thank you, Lord.

August 5, 2003   Proved Myself to You Again

Lord, I thank you for your grace, mercies, your angels that encamp around and about me. As I was coming home from work today on Rt 280, a car hit my car from behind. The impact was so strong that it flung my car a great distance. My co-worker and I received some injuries, but we're still here by your grace and mercy. The enemy meant it for bad, but God, I believe you're working and will work it out for my good. *(Note: I no longer believe those bad things happen for our good. 11/18)*

As I drove home after the accident, Lord, you said, *"I've proved myself to you again."* Lord, that was enough for me to praise and thank you because truly, you've proven yourself to me once again.

August 6, 2003 — Happy Birthday to my Baby

Today, my baby girl celebrates her 9th birthday. Lord, I thank you so much for keeping and prospering, Lexi. Lord, nine means fruitfulness, harvest, fruition, and deliverance. I pray, oh Lord, that you would bring about all these things and more in her life. And Lord, I pray **1 Chronicles 4:10** over Alexia's life.

It states, "**And Jabez called on the God of Israel, saying, Oh that thou wouldest bless me indeed, and enlarge my coast, and that thine hand might be with me, and that thou wouldest keep me from evil, that it may not grieve me! And God granted him that which he requested.**"

Father, I pray that you would bless Alexia and enlarge her coast and that your hand might be with and on her. I pray that you would keep her from evil, that it will not grieve her. In Jesus' name. As I think back about yesterday, how the devil tried to kill me, but for God!!!

August 18, 2003 — Late in The Midnight Hour

Holy Spirit, it's 12:25 a.m. So much has happened, but despite it all, I thank you, Lord, because surely you haven't left Lexi and me. Neither have you forsaken us and for that, I thank you.

September 13, 2003 — Childhood Boyfriend

Good morning, Father, Son, and Holy Ghost. Thank you for another day. Lord, lately, I've been thinking more about being married. You know my requests where a husband is concerned. Of course, there's room for exception. I often think about (we'll call him Asher) my Childhood boyfriend.

What is he doing? Is he married? Does he have children? I don't know what he's like, but I hope he's saved. Asher would probably be the only short (if he is) Jamaican man I would marry. I hope to see him again someday and hope that it will be as though we were kids again when that day comes. I hope that he remembers me and thinks about me as I do him.

October 11, 2003 — My Birthday

It's my birthday, I have a dinner date planned, but I must say I am quite sad. I have always been sad on my birthday, and I pray for the day when the Lord will manifest the answers to my prayers.

Thank you, Lord, for another year.

October 22, 2003 — Lord, please help!

I've been so angry, frustrated, tired, and fed up for the past few weeks. So much has been going on, and I still can't find a dance school for Lexi that would work with her on her level. I love my job, but the pay is low. I need a job that will start me off with at least $40K per year. Lord, please help!

October 27, 2003 — You Kept Me

Lord, my God, father, king, Savior, deliverer, redeemer, comfort, peace, joy, strong tower, and refuge. My bondage breaker, my very present help in the time of trouble. I choose to submit. I love you, Lord, for in submitting to you, I will be able to resist the devil, and he shall flee.

Lord, when I have no one else to turn to, you are there. Father, amid everything, you've kept me. When you didn't deliver, heal, answer, restore, avenge, bring and show up when I wanted you to, but in your own time, Lord, even then, you kept me. And for that, Lord, I thank you.

Thank you, Lord, for always being there. Lord, you said in your word that you would never leave me or forsake me. Lord, at times, I feel as if you're nowhere around; it feels as if you're not here or there. Lord, even then, you've been there, and Lord, I thank you. Thank you for keeping me.

Lord, when I could have lost my mind, you kept me. When my heart hurt so badly, and I just wanted to take it out, you kept me. Lord, when I wanted you to take Lexi and me home, you kept me and said,

"*Not so, my daughter. I have work for you to do.*" Lord, you kept me. Lord, when I was in those accidents, and the enemy wanted to kill Lexi and me, you kept us. When I was lying on the doctor's table having surgery, and when I was given anesthesia to go to sleep, Lord, even then, you kept me.

Lord, I could have been dead and gone and left my sweet precious Lexi, but Lord, you kept me. When I could have gotten STD, Lord, you kept me. When the enemy came to steal, kill, and destroy, Lord, you kept me. When the devil used, abused me, and threw me to the side, Lord, even then, you picked me up, brushed me off, washed me in your blood.

Thank you, Lord, that you kept me. So, Lord, I thank you that, when I have no one else to talk to but you, I can come and pour out my heart to you. Lord, I thank you that you kept me!! I love you, Lord.

November 20, 2003 — Thankful

My Lord and my king, I'm crying, and it's not because my heart is broken over a man, or because you didn't answer my prayer, it's not because I want something, but God, it's because you've been good. Father, you're faithful to your word to perform it. Because, when I think about all that you've done, you kept Lexi and me, Lord, I thank you. I love you for your grace and mercy.

November 30, 2003 — My Ways Are Prosperous

I fell asleep on my knees as I was praying. Lord, you spoke the following words into my spirit as I woke. *"Your ways are prosperous"* **Psalm 119**. Thank you, Lord.

December 1, 2003 — Work of My Hand Is Blessed

In my quiet and devotional time, one of the scriptures that touched my heart more than the others was **Psalm 138:8 The Lord will perfect that which concerns me; thy mercy O Lord, endureth forever: forsake not the works of thine own hand.** Thank you, Lord.

December 12, 2003 — I Am Humble

In my Devotional time, **1 Peter 5:5** stood out to me. It states, "Likewise, ye younger, submit yourselves unto the elder. Yea, all of you be subject one to another, and be clothed with humility: for God resisteth the proud, and giveth grace to the humble." Thank you, Lord.

December 12, 2003 — Sweet Sleep

In my daily scripture reading, this beautiful portion of scripture stood out to me. Thank you, Lord, that even in your written word you speak.

Proverbs 3:24-26 [24] **When thou liest down, thou shalt not be afraid: yea, thou shalt lie down, and thy sleep shall be sweet.** [25] **Be not afraid of sudden fear, neither of the desolation of the wicked, when it cometh.** [26] **For the Lord shall be thy confidence, and shall keep thy foot from being taken.**

December 4, 2003 — Uncommon Blessings

It's 1 a.m. Father, I just want to thank you for your grace and mercy that is new every morning. Thank you for your word that is true, instructs, and guides me. As I woke this morning, the uncommon blessings were running in my spirit, heart, mind, soul, and natural and spiritual ear.

The Harvest of Uncommon Blessings:

1. Wisdom
2. Favor
3. Health and healing
4. Ideas
5. Financial prosperity
6. Family restoration
7. My promotion

Plus, all the others: I claim them all for my family and myself in Jesus' name. Prayer: Father, thank you for manifesting the uncommon blessing in my life and Lexi's. I bind the enemy, and I rebuke you in Jesus' name. I command you to take your hands off my blessings in Jesus' name. Father, dispatch the ministering angels and cause the blessings to come to my household in Jesus' name. I receive and believe in Jesus' name.

December 5, 2003 — Sudden Destruction?

As I awoke, I heard the Lord say, "Fear not." In my time of prayer, as I waited on the Lord, he impressed upon my spirit *"sudden destruction."* **1 Thessalonians 5:3 For when they shall say, Peace and safety; then sudden destruction cometh upon them, as travail upon a woman with child; and they shall not escape.**

Father, I pray for Lexi and me that you will protect and keep us safe. I pray for people and our nation in Jesus' name. I bind the hands of the enemy in Jesus' name.

December 6, 2003 — Living Waters

Throughout last night, I was talking to the Lord about **Psalm 51**, where the psalmist asks the Lord to create in him a clean heart of God.

As I prayed, I heard, *"Living waters shall flow forth."* Thank you, Lord, for your word. Thank you for the living waters manifesting in Lexi's and my life. Father, I pray that you will create a clean heart and renew the right spirit within me.

January 1, 2004 — A Shake Up

The end of one year and the beginning of a new one. A new opportunity to live my life and Lexi's life for the Lord. I'm feeling a shakeup in my spirit, but Lord, I thank you for your keeping power.

Father, thank you that you hold Lexi and me in the palm of your hand, and no one or nothing can pluck us out. Thank you for new opportunities, new blessings, and favor.

January 8, 2004 — The Sound of The Snow

Thank you, Lord, for a new year. You dropped the following word for this season in my heart. *"Listen to the sound of the snow."*

April 12, 2004 — Manifestation of the Tithe

Lord, I need you to help me with my finances. Manifest your blessings of the tithe in my life. Please help me to get a social life so that you can send my husband to find me. Thank you, Lord, and please manifest your blessings in our lives.

April 14, 2004 — Thank You

Somewhere between last night and this morning, as I awoke, I heard these words, *"God, my God, why has thou forsaken me?"* These were the last words Jesus spoke on the cross before giving up the ghost. Thank you, Lord.

Father, in the name of Jesus, I thank you for bringing Lexi and me out and in. Thank you for peace today at work and home. Thank you that the car tire could go out and come back without me putting air in it. Thank you, Lord.

April 15, 2004 — Stay In

As I awoke this morning, I heard the word *"forgiveness,"* and I dreamt **Matthew 7**. Thank you, Lord.

My first job out of college was the first one I interviewed for, and I accepted it because I needed to provide shelter and food for Alexia and me. It was a social service agency where we helped disabled adults participate in community events.

Father, I thank you that I could stay inside at work today and that tomorrow is payday. Thank you, Lord.

April 16, 2004 — Thank you for Payday

Father, thank you that I got paid today.

April 17, 2004 — Thank You for $50

Father, thank you for leading me to go to Piscataway today. I was able to pray for Mr. Waters, and you allowed Thelma to bless me with $50.00 for my graduation. Thank you!

April 17, 2004 #2 — Open Trunk

Thank you for the Prophetic Dinner. Thank you for leading me to go back outside to get the food. It happened that I drove from Jersey City with my trunk open, so in going back out to get the food, I saw that it was open.

Thank you that I didn't have to buy the juice because someone already purchased it, and thank you for giving Alexia and me the strength to press towards the mark. Strengthen us; I pray continually.

April 18, 2004 — You Must Survive

Lord, I thank you for a blessed time in church. We were small; nevertheless, you blessed us. While standing at the pulpit, you impressed upon my heart that I must survive Faith Christian Center. If I do, I can make it anywhere and in the ministry. Thank you, Lord.

April 18, 2004 #2 — U-Turn

Lord, I thank you for protecting Lexi and me from having that accident. A young man ran the stop sign, and I almost ran into him, but the Holy Spirit redirected my hands so that I made a U-turn instead.

Thank you, Lord, for your angels that encamp around us and that no weapon formed against us shall prosper. I thank you that you uphold us in your hand and that nothing or no one can pluck us out. Thank you that your grace and mercy endure forever!

April 19, 2004 — Favor

Thank you, Lord, that I woke up with, *"Let everything that has breath praise the Lord,"* in my heart. Thank you! I am thankful that work was peaceful, and thank you for your favor at the air pump.

Thank you for showing me favor with Al, my boss, and Lux, my landlord, and for sowing a seed in my book table.

April 20, 2004 — Safety

Thank you, Lord, for a blessed day for bringing us out and bringing us back home safely.

April 21, 2004 — More Favor

Today, I went to court because of the man who hit my car and said he didn't do it, even though we saw him. He pled guilty to a lesser charge.

Lord, I thank you for your favor with the insurance company to pay for the damages to my car, and I thank you also for Pastor Bradshaw, who blessed me with $200.00 for my book table.

April 22, 2004 — Favor Again

Thank you, Lord, that you brought Alexia through the MRI under sedation. The social worker also informed me that we have an interview with the school that I am trying to get Alexia in. Thank you, Lord.

Thank you for **James 1:13-14. **[13]** Let no man say when he is tempted, I am tempted of God: for God cannot be tempted with evil, neither tempteth he any man:** [14]** But every man is tempted, when he is drawn away of his own lust, and enticed.**

April 23, 2004 — Vengeance Belongs to the Lord

Thank you today, Lord, for work. You see and know what's going on, and I thank you for avenging me of my adversaries. Thank you for working it out.

Thank you for, **1 John 1:9 If we confess our sins, he is faithful and just to forgive us our sins, and to cleanse us from all unrighteousness.**

April 24, 2004 — Winner

Today, Lexi and I went to a computer workshop, and we won a computer! Thank you, Lord, because I needed one, and you worked it all out. Thank you, Jesus.

April 25, 2004 — A Servant's Heart

Thank you, Lord, for a blessed day in the church today. In our afternoon service, I served my Bishop, Marvin Bradshaw Sr., which gives me great pleasure and blessing. Thank you, Lord.

April 26, 2004 — Victory

Thank you for work today. Thank you for removing my enemies and working out every situation. Thank you, Lord.

April 27, 2004 — Renewed Strength

Father, thank you for dropping in my spirit, **Isaiah 40:30-31** [30] **Even the youths shall faint and be weary, and the young men shall utterly fall:** [31] **But they that wait upon the Lord shall renew their strength; they shall mount up with wings as eagles; they shall run, and not be weary; and they shall walk, and not faint.**

Father God, I thank you that you always have a "now" word for me. Thank you for speaking to me whenever I need to hear from you. Thank you for encouraging me as you did, Joshua. Thank you for renewing my strength like the eagles.

April 28, 2004 — Faithful

Proverbs 28:20 A faithful man shall abound with blessings: but he that maketh haste to be rich shall not be innocent.

Thank you, Lord, that I am faithful. Thank you for giving me the grace and the strength to continue to be faithful in Jesus' name.

April 29, 2004 — God in the Beginning

Genesis 1:1 In the beginning God...

Read that again, slowly. In the beginning, God... Thank you, Lord, that in the beginning, you were present. So, you will never leave me alone or forsake me because you will always be there for Lexi and me. Thank you, Lord!

April 30, 2004 — In the Image of God

Genesis 1:26 And God said, Let us make man in our image, after our likeness: and let them have dominion over the fish of the sea, and over the fowl of the air, and over the cattle, and over all the earth, and over every creeping thing that creepeth upon the earth.

Father, I thank you for making me in your image, after your likeness. Thank you that I have dominion over the earth. Therefore, I speak peace into the world of my life. I speak health, wealth, blessings, prosperity, and long life. I call forth my husband. I call my children blessed to a thousand generations.

I curse every sickness, disease, lack, curse, and everything that is not like you. I speak the blessing over Lexi's and my life, that of a husband, children, family, and friends. I declare that I am blessed, and I have everything I need in Jesus' name.

May 16, 2004 — Bless Me Indeed

As I woke, I heard the spirit of the Lord say, *"You have not because you asked not."* So, Lord, I ask you for everything that Lexi and I need. Lord, help me be consistent in my time of studying and communion with you in Jesus' name.

June 10, 2004 — Show Me What to Do

Lord, thank you for your forgiveness. Thank you for the blood of Jesus Christ. I am reminded of **2 Chronicles 20:3 And Jehoshaphat feared, set himself to seek the Lord, and proclaimed a fast throughout Judah.**

Jehoshaphat proclaimed a fast because he needed to hear from you about what he should do about his enemies. Thank you, Lord, for showing me what to do.

July 26, 2004 — My Mother in the Faith

Lord, my heart is breaking for my mother in the faith, First Lady Edna Bradshaw, and this situation. Bless her, strengthen her, guide her, and protect her. Thank you for all that she has taught me. I love that she has always known the type of husband I desire. When guys came to the church and claimed that they would marry me, she would laugh because we both knew what I wanted.

August 6, 2004 — My Baby's Birthday

Today is my baby's girl's birthday. I speak a blessing over Alexia's life. Father, you see and know everything we have been through with the learning disability and cognitive impairment. But father, I thank you for keeping us and strengthening us. Thank you for making a way out of no way for us. I speak a blessing over Alexia's life. Lexi is blessed going and coming. Lexi loves the Lord with all her heart, mind, soul, and body.

I declare that Lexi will live for the Lord all the days of her life, and she will never depart or turn away. Lexi is saved and filled with the Holy Ghost. All of Alexia's needs are met according to your riches in glory by Christ Jesus. I declare that Lexi is the healed of the Lord, from the crown of her head to the very soles of her feet. Lexi has everything she needs, and all her needs are met. Lexi lacks no good thing.

Thank you for blessing Lexi with godly teachers and friends. Thank you that, as she rides on the school bus, the angels of the Lord surround Lexi and her buses. They encamp around her and protect her from all harm and danger, both seen and unseen. Thank you for getting Lexi into the school to help her grow and blossom. I thank you that she can stay until she is 21 years old. Thank you for showing her favor with her teachers, principals, and everyone who works with her.

I thank you that Lexi is a godly, obedient, and respectful child. I thank you for blessing Lexi from the crown of her head to the very soles of her feet. Lord, you have good plans for Lexi. Plans to prosper her and give her an expectant end. We expect greatness, increase, guidance, protection, a long, happy, healthy, and blessed life. We expect you to crown her with peace and blessings and the Uncommon blessings manifestation. In Jesus' name!! I call it done in Jesus' name, amen.

August 11, 2004 — Time to Move On

I need to move on from this brother who showed interest in me. I was somewhat interested but based on the information I learned about him. I don't think he's right for me. He's not the man for me. Can I carry a marriage alone? No! In relationships, there must be compromises, give, and take. There's so much I want from God. So much I desire in my Boaz-my man of God, the high priest of my house, someone who loves God and can love and accept my daughter as his own.

I desire a praying and fasting man who reads and studies the word of God. A man that can stand up and take charge. A mature and understanding man, full of love and compassion. I desire a man that is sociable and polite. Someone who will make me laugh, who will stick with me in the good and bad times, no matter what we go through or what comes or goes, but will stand still and see the salvation of the Lord.

I desire a man of God who will fight for me, fight for us, our marriage, and family. A man who will declare that he knows that I am the woman for him will not allow anything or anyone to tear us apart. Father, I pray that you will send my Boaz now in Jesus' name.

Moments of Gratitude

November 19, 2004 — *An Innocent Child*

Today, we laid Maria's son, Paul, to rest. Lord, it was so sad! One of the most painful days of my life. I feel as if a part of me died like he was my child. I pray that you will strengthen, bless, keep, and heal Maria's, broken heart. Take away the pain that she feels and help her find peace in you.

Thank you for the life of Paul. I am sure he is resting with the Lord, and we will see him again. Thank you for healing the brokenness in his mother's heart and life, and may you give her peace and comfort during this time.

November 25, 2004 — *Thanksgiving*

Lord, I thank you for your goodness and your mercy. As I look back on my Thank You Journal's last entry, the last thing I thanked you for was moving my enemies. I'm thankful that you've moved them from my job, and I'm now the assistant manager. Lord, on this Thanksgiving Day, I thank you!

I thank you for "YOU." Thank you, Father, for the Lord Jesus Christ and the Holy Spirit. Thank you, Lord, for sending Jesus Christ, the manifestation of the Father, Son, and Holy Ghost. Father, you gave your son for me and for this world, to die for our past, present, and future sins.

When I think about it, what can I say but *"Thank you, Lord!"* You've been there for Alexia and me. You've kept us, provided, guided, and watched over us. Thank you that you've protected, directed, blessed, and loved us. You have delivered, set us free, taught, disciplined, comforted, healed, and held us. God, you've been there for Lexi and me, and I will forever be grateful. THANK YOU, LORD!

There are so many people I'm thankful for, Lord: Alexia, she's been such a blessing to me, and, God, you've been blessing me through her. You've shown her favor in her new school. She's been blessed at church. You've called her to the office of the Pastor, and you've already begun to use her mightily. Lord, I thank you!

Father, I thank you for the many mothers you've blessed Alexia and me with over the years. Mom Waters, Ms. Mervis, Mom Caddle, Sis. Edna Bradshaw, Ms. Owens, Sis. Hodge-Jackson, Pastor Harris, Prophetess Jackson, and over all these years, you've blessed me with a father in the faith, Bishop Marvin Bradshaw Sr.

Because of Bishop Bradshaw, I've learned so much: my love for God and the scriptures, my desire to study and expound upon the scriptures, my passion, and my compassion for people. And father, even though I'm not at FCC anymore, I love Pastor Bradshaw and will always love him because he's my daddy, and that's where I got my foundation about the things of God.

Even though you didn't see it fit to bless me with any biological sisters, you've blessed me with three sisters, Jacqueline, Jenifer, and Rachel. Nevertheless, it's Jacky who has blessed me more than ever. She's my friend. We laugh and cry together, pray together, help each other with our children, and we're there for each other through different avenues. And, Lord, I thank you for my co-worker's friends and associates.

Thank you for deaconesses Grace and Shawn, for Dee, Philomena, Lorraine, Claudette, and Victoria. Thank you for the ARC and my clients at LCRC. Thank you for my ability to work for those less fortunate, and thank you for Evon and her family.

Thank you for Katrina, Al, Latricia, Brian, and my many associates at Rutgers University. Thank you for David, Kenyatta, and Robert. Thank you for the School of The Prophets. Thanks for this apartment, and thank you for showing us favor with the landlord. Thank you for blessing and making Alexia and me prosperous in every area of our lives. Thank you, Lord, and WE LOVE YOU, LORD!

December 25, 2004 — Christmas

Lord, I thank you for the Lord Jesus Christ. Today is the day that was chosen to celebrate our Lord's birth. If He wasn't born, then He couldn't have died, rose and ascended to sit on the right hand of the father, and for that, I thank you!

December 31, 2004 — Reflection

The old year is slowly passing away, and the New Year is speedily approaching. Full of promises, blessings, new opportunities, and excitement. Lord, when I look over this year and see all that you've done, all that you've brought me through, I can't help but say, *"THANK YOU!"*

When I was sick, lying on the doctor's table, you were there! When I was hurt and disappointed in myself, you encouraged me! When I was making one of the most important decisions of my life, and which job to accept, Lord, you were there. When I was bawling on my futon, crying out to you, you encouraged me with the song, *"I need you more today than I did yesterday."* Lord, I thank you.

This year has been one of the most hurtful, painful, and worst years of my life, but God, I thank you for bringing me out!! THANK YOU, LORD!

January 1, 2005 — Grace

2005 is the year of *GRACE!* 2005 is my year of grace, mercy, and blessings. I speak the blessings in my and Alexia's lives. 2005 is our year of prosperity, peace, breakthrough, abundance, and all the blessings God has in store for us. Thank you, Lord!

March 5, 2005 — Feeling Abandoned

Today, as I drove on Clinton Avenue, Lord, I felt abandoned by you. Things are not exactly coming together for me, even though I know you said you would never leave or forsake me. As I look through my journal, I notice that it's been a while since I took the time to write down my thank you for your grace and mercy.

If anyone should be feeling abandoned, it should be you by me. Not that I haven't been praying, reading, and studying the scriptures or spending quality time with you because of all these things I've been doing. I just haven't been writing them down. Please forgive me, Lord.

Lord, I need you to come through for Lexi and me, new job, finances, car, family, ministry, my husband, etc. Father, I know that, in due time, you'll come through for us. Lord, just give me the strength and patience to come through this time and endure in Jesus' name. Lord, I thank you for that new job that I need. Thank you for showing me favor and making a way out of no way. I love you, Lord.

July 4, 2005 — It's Coming Back

"What goes around comes around." Lord, isn't it something that what goes around comes around? Thank you for your grace and favor upon my life and Lexi's.

August 1, 2005 — Thank You for a New Job

Lord, my grace for this job has worn out. I thank you for blessing me with a new job. I love the people. However, it's time for me to move on. I have had the paperwork to get a job with the state since I left school, and I will go ahead and see what's available.

August 6, 2005 — Precious Gift

Lord, today is my baby's birthday. Thank you for all that you've done in her life and for all that you're doing in and through her. You've anointed her, blessed her, increased her, and shown her favor in school and church. Lord, I thank you that Lexi is so beautiful inside and out. Lexi is godly, obedient, honorable, and respectful. Thank you that Lexi has found favor everywhere she goes and with everyone she meets.

I pray the blessing continues over her life and that you bless her. I declare that all her needs are met in Jesus' name. She needs no good thing. You go out with her, and you come in with her. Alexia shall be the head and not the tail. She shall be only above and not below. Lord, you manifest your love and your presence to her. Thank you for dispatching your ministering angels to watch over her and protect her.

Thank you for saying that you would always be with Lexi and never leave or forsake her. You are with her when she's on her school bus and in school, and at play. You will be with her forever and ever, and your peace will keep her and bless her. Thank you, Lord!

September 1, 2005 — I Have It

Lord, I thank you for leading me to fill out the paperwork for the job with the state. The test is coming up, and I believe in you for the victory I have in Jesus' name.

Janice Hylton Thompson

October 5, 2005 *Missing Out*

(Note: I remember writing this. This was a sorrowful time in my life.)

My father, I wanted to write to you last night, but I couldn't find my journal. So, here I am. Lord, about 12-12:30 a.m. last night, I began to think. Think that in a few days, I'll be 28 years old. Ever since I was 16, I've been a mom, then a college student, then an employee.

And I've been so busy doing those things that I didn't enjoy my teenage years. I was always responsible, never really got to lie around and relax, watch T.V. until 4 or 5 in the morning, or just wake up with no cares in the world.

Lord, what do I do? Sometimes, I just want to sit around and chill and do nothing, no cares, no responsibility. Well, I'm 28, a mom of an 11-year-old special needs child, an employee, minister, and other things. And I'm ashamed to say that I've been lazy about it as far as ministry is concerned. I just want the pieces of my life to come together. I am presently at SOP in Newark, and so far, it's all good. I need a new job with better pay, time, benefits, etc. Daddy, sometimes I feel as if I'm too needy.

And Father, my sweet and precious Lexi, bless my baby, Lord, and keep her. Lexi is the head and not the tail. She shall be above only and not beneath in Jesus' name. Bless my family and save my loved ones in Jesus' name. Thank you, and I love you, Lord.

October 9, 2005 — A Clean Heart

Good morning, Father. This morning, around 6 a.m., you dropped in my heart, the desperate plead of King David **Psalm 51:10**. Create in me a clean heart and renew the right spirit within me. This is what I need. Over the last few weeks, I've been angry, upset, agitated, aggravated, irritated, and temperamental. I feel as if I've been unhappy and discontented.

On 10/11, two days from today, I will be 28, and as I lay down thinking about what I wrote on the last page, it hit me that it's time for me to grow up. Time for me to stop living in the past. I didn't enjoy my teenage years, so I'm angry and upset about that.

Things didn't go well in my life, so I've been down about it. The past is the past, and it has helped me be a better woman, mother, and daughter of the King. So, Lord, I thank you for seeing me through it all.

October 10, 2005 — Birthday Dates

A few guys asked me out for my birthday, but I decided that I would not do that anymore. My birthday is special and should not be spent with folks who are not special to me. So, no more dates on my birthday. My birthday is reserved for Mr. Boaz, my family, and my friends.

October 11, 2005 — Give Thanks

Lord, thank you for sparing my life to see another birthday. Why am I so sad? Lord, I thank you for waking me up. Thank you for this birthday. Thank you for Lexi. Thank you that we are healthy and wealthy, nothing broken or missing. Thank you for the activity of our limbs. We can see, hear, talk, smell, feel, walk, wash, and feed ourselves.

Lord, as I open my cabinets, I see that we have food in them. My fridge has pre-made food. Thank you for the heat and this beautiful and cozy apartment. Thank you for the clothes, shoes, coats, socks, and gorgeous dresses.

Thank you that I can take off work for my birthday because I refuse to work on my birthday. Thank you, Lord, that today is a day of reflection and thanksgiving, despite my circumstances. Thank you, Lord, for another year! And Lord, I thank you for anointing me to write my first published book, *Praying for Our Children*. I declare that it will be the number 1 best seller.

October 11, 2005 — Birthday Dinner

Lord, thank you for my birthday dinner tonight with my god mom Sister Hodge, a few other church friends, and my baby girl. I cried like a baby. You know, I've realized that my birthdays are incredibly sad for me. I just need things to begin to work for Lexi and me. And yes, yes, Lord, I want to be married. I want my husband. Thank you for the ladies encouraging me that, in time, the Lord will bless me with my husband and for me to be grateful and happy for all that you have done.

Today, on my 28th birthday, I decided to be happy, thankful, and wait patiently for you to manifest my blessing. I have a test coming up soon for that new job that will double what I earn now. Thank you, Lord, that I receive it in Jesus' name.

And Lord, I speak the blessings of the Lord over my life. I declare that I am a goodly woman and mom. I am anointed and appointed for such a time as this. I thank you that I am anointed to write, teach, and preach your word. I thank you that many people will be blessed, encouraged, healed, and delivered by the words you give me to write. I declare that I am an anointed writer. My heart and ears are tuned into the Holy Spirit, and I will write what thus says the Lord.

I thank you for blessing me with my Boaz, now in Jesus' name. I declare that he is saved, filled with the Holy Spirit, and is a man who can lead and be the light in our home. I declare and decree that we can submit to each other. I declare that my husband is a good man who will provide a comfortable life for Lexi, himself, me, and our household.

I pray for my husband now, and I declare and decree that, in due time, he will find me. I pray that his heart is tuned into you, that he is keeping himself for me as I am keeping myself for him. Bless my Boaz, Lord, and may you guide and protect him as only you can.

I pray that we will not attach to anyone that is not your will. I bind the hands of the enemy, and I thank you for your guidance in Jesus' name. When we see each other, I pray that there will be an instant connection between us. I call it done in Jesus' name, Amen.

October 20, 2005 — Reflection

Father, it's been a while since I wrote in this journal because I have been spending more time writing my books. Not that I haven't had anything to thank you for because, God, you've been good.

You've kept Lexi and me. You've provided and spared our lives another year; you've given me a revelation about the things I need to work on in my life. You've been good to me, and Father, I thank you. Lord, not only will this be a 'thank you book,' but it will also be a book of my deepest cry to you, a book of prayer.

October 30, 2005 — Healing the Father's Fracture

Dear Father, it's 12:29 a.m., and Pastor Dickow Gregory just finished teaching on *"Healing the Father's Fracture."* This is ironic because I thought that I didn't have a father in my life to teach me about men until I met my spiritual father, Pastor Bradshaw when I was about seventeen.

Pastor Dickow was teaching about knowing God as a father. I was always searching for that father figure. That's why I need to be in a church where the pastor is a real man because I need that.

I need that father figure or example in my life. I think back to when my church split. It was so painful for me during that time. I realized that I needed to get to know you as Father. When I pray, I say father but rarely ever call you *"daddy."* And Father, that's who you are. You are my daddy.

I guess that's why I didn't care for any of the guys that were interested in me. I saw them as little boys versus real men. Father, I desire my Boaz, someone who can be an example, a saved, sanctify and Holy Ghost-filled, fire baptized, tongue talking, loving God with all of his heart, mind, soul, and body, a man of God.

Someone who can be a father to Lexi, love her, take her as his own, treat her right, won't abuse, molest, rape, or fondle her but treat her as a daughter of the king. A man who will love Lexi and me and provide for us, be the priest of our home, be an example as Sarah called Abraham Lord or daddy.

My father, daddy, I don't want Alexia going through the same things I went through, struggling with guys, not having a father figure, etc. So, Father, I yield to you for you to teach me how to love, respect, and treat a man of God, my Boaz, so that when you send him into my life, I will do him right. Help me, Father, deal with my heart's issues and teach Alexia in Jesus' name.

Please help me, Father, stop living in the past and struggling. Help me to deal with the issues in my past. Please help me to have the right attitude, spirit, respect, and honor. Please give me the strength to listen to you without getting upset or angry, to listen and take heed. From this moment forward, I'm through living in the past, and I'm looking forward to a future of higher heights and deeper depths in Jesus' name. Thank you, Lord.

October 31, 2005 — A Simple Prayer

Lord, please renew my heart. Thank you, Lord, that you still answer prayers.

November 1, 2005 — $.03 Cents Praise

Lord, thank you that I felt led to go to a gas station. I went to another one because it was closer to Alexia's school. I went there, and it was closed, so I went back to the one I was going to go to initially, and the gas price was $2.29 for regular. But as I pulled up, the gas attendant was changing the price to $2.26. Thank you, Lord.

November 5, 2005 — Protection

Father, in the name of Jesus, I thank you for this: I was going to a concert, and my tire was flat. Thank you for leading us there, and then back and to the tire shop where I needed a new tire. But I thank you that I had a spare.

November 6, 2005 — Small Blessings

Today, I thank you that I saw Ms. Elyse and dropped her off, and I talked with her a little about the Lord. Thank you for the small things.

November 9, 2005 — Gifts Will Make Room

I thank you, Lord, that I was able to get up by your strength and seek your face. Thank you, Father, that as I prayed about the ministry and walked into the bathroom, I opened my mouth, and you filled it with these words. *"My gift will make room for me!"* Thank you, Lord, that my writing and teaching gift will make room for me.

November 10, 2005 — Safety

Thank you, Lord, for bringing us out and bringing us back in. Your guardian angels were watching over us and keeping us safe in their arms. Thank you, Lord.

November 11, 2005 — I Will Fill It

Daddy, thank you for this day off from work. Thank you for watching over Lexi and me. Father, thank you for the vision of a home for girls. Thank you for the dream and vision, and thank you for bringing it to pass.

Thank you for the vision for my ministry, which includes community programs. Lord, it has been over eight years that you've given me these visions of ministry, and thank you for trusting me with it.

November 12, 2005 — Daddy

As I read over my entry from yesterday, I saw that I called you Daddy. Lord, this has been a long journey, but I thank you that you are continually healing me, where I can comfortably call you Daddy, my Abba father. Thank you, Lord. (See my book, *Abba Father*, coming soon.)

November 24, 2005 — Write the Vision

Father, I was praying in tongues, and you laid on my heart **Isaiah 61** for Lexi about giving her Beauty for Ashes, and you laid on my heart to get a prayer journal. Thank you, Lord.

I thought I could use this book, but this is my 'Thank You Journal/Book,' no requests. The only thing I'm going to put in this book is THANK YOU, LORD.

December 14, 2005 — I Love You, Lord

I am so looking forward to God manifesting my husband! But in the meantime, Lord, I love you so much. You've been so good to me. You have loved, covered, and beautified me. Your grace and mercy are from everlasting to everlasting, and your love for me will never change. Thank you, Lord.

December 31, 2005 — I Want A Husband

So, Mion asked me to marry him. I said no. First, he isn't even the type of man I would marry. He is way younger than I am, and I want a father figure for Lexi, not a boy she can have a crush on. He is childish, such a child. Plus, he can't even provide for himself, much less for Lexi and me. He still lives at home, sharing a room with his brother. So, where exactly are we going to live?

Nope, I want a real and true man of God. One that can provide and protect and profess his love for me. He doesn't seem to be interested in the things of God, no zeal or passion at all. I had to wonder if he could be the head of my home, a man I could honor, respect, and turn my life over to, who could be a father figure for Lexi. I wondered if he could go with me on my journey and help me fulfill God's will and destiny for my life.

He proposed to a friend from home, and she accepted. He had said I could rescue him and save him by accepting his proposal. I told him no because I would be rescuing him forever, and that's not the type of man or marriage that I want. Well, his new fiancé forbids him to speak to me, which is fine with me. But, Lord, I just want to thank you that I have always known what I want in a husband.

And I thank you for your grace and mercy that I can stand still on my heart's desire. I pray for my brother, though, that your will be done in his life. When I woke up, the Lord gave me **2 Samuel 12:14-24**

January 1, 2006 — New Beginnings

A happy and blessed new year to Lexi and me. Things are beginning to look up for us. I am looking forward to my new job! Thank you, Lord, for opening the door and blessing me with favor. I look forward to meeting new people, having new opportunities, and learning new things.

Also, Lord, I thank you for laying on my heart to write down the things I desire in my husband. Understanding that some things are ongoing, as I wrote this entry, I began to laugh because I remember about a month ago, I saw this guy that my godmother tried to hook me up with. We talked for a while, and then it just dried up on its own.

Now that was years ago. He was a bit older than me, a firefighter, and saved. But if I remember correctly, he was cheap. He never asked me out but wanted me to invite him over for dinner. I'm in no rush, but I'm going to rest in the Lord and wait for the Lord to work things out for me.

Thank you, Lord, and I trust you for the victory in every aspect of my life. I love you, and I appreciate you for all that you do for Lexi and me.

January 22, 006 — I Have the Victory

Yesterday morning, when I came home from New Year's Eve service, I had such a burden for singles who want to get married. My heart was heavy and aching, and while I was in service, I was holding my heart down. A sister came to me and said, "You have the victory. You are victorious, both you and your family..."

A confirmation that, as before I went to church, the Lord spoke to me and said, *"You have the victory and take authority over your emotions."* The enemy has been attacking my thoughts lately, but the Lord told me, *"When you pray, believe that you've received that which you've prayed for."*

When I came home from the New Year Eve Service, my heart was still heavy. I laid on the floor, talked to the Lord, and poured out my soul before him. When I woke up this morning, I felt a release in my spirit and heart. That burden and heaviness of my aching heart were gone, and I thank you, Lord.

January 3, 2006   *The Purpose Driven Life*

Lord, thank you that today I will begin to read *The Purpose Driven Life* by Rick Warren. One of the things that got my attention was, "Whenever God wanted to prepare someone for his purpose, he took 40 days." Lord, I feel it in my spirit that good is about to come to my baby girl and me. Thank you, Lord.

January 9, 2006   *God Brought Me Out*

I remember being in church on 1/1/06, and the Elder, during us praising God, said, "God brought you out." At that moment, there was a breakthrough in my spirit. God brought me out of only he-knows-what. Father, a few things you dropped in my spirit:
1. Why I'm hurting again
2. It's dead

3. Give it up for the Kingdom of God
4. I brought you out
5. Again, give it up for the kingdom of God.

Lord, only you know what you kept me from and brought me out of. I thank you, my Lord, my God, my father. Thank you, Lord.

January 12, 2006 — *I Want You, Lord*

Father, I want to thank you for your grace and mercy. Today, I realized that I want you more than anything else: more than a husband, more than that job that I'm waiting to come through, or anything else I desire. I want more of you, Father.

Father, I want you the creator, and then you will bless me with your creation. Thank you, father. I thought of Ruth, Jesus, Esther, Abraham, who gave up the creation for the creator, and in the end, you blessed them tremendously. Ruth gave up what she knew for Naomi's faith, and she became the great-grandmother of Jesus. Jesus didn't think of himself but saw all humanity and submitted to God. Jesus is our great mediator and is seated on the Father's right hand.

Abraham stepped out in faith and trusted God, and became the father of faith. Esther, a Jewish girl, became a queen. Father, I choose to go after you. I want you with all my heart, mind, soul, and body. For once in a long time, I felt a release and peace in my spirit. And in the words of my father in the faith, Pastor Marvin Bradshaw Sr, "ALL IS WELL." In Jesus' name and thank you, Lord.

January 13, 2006 — God Is Working in Me

Father, I thank you for speaking to me. While I was waiting for Lexi's bus, I felt in my spirit that you were saying, "I have work to do in your life. I'm ready to move in your life, and I'm not going to allow anything or anyone to keep my will and plan for your life from coming to pass in your life."

Lord, I thank you. Do it in me, through me, and for me. I put all my hope, trust, and faith in you. God, I want you more than anything or anyone else. You said in **Matthew 6:33** to seek first the kingdom of God and all your righteousness, and you would add all the things I need in my life. Thank you, Lord, and I love you.

January 22, 2006 — Waiting to Hear

I'm waiting to hear about this new job. I thank you for it, and I receive it in Jesus' name. On 1/18/06, I went to a CVS, working as a secret shopper to earn extra income to take care of Lexi and me, and it was tough to find parking at this store. I passed the store looking for parking, but thankfully, I eventually found a space.

As soon as I get this new job and complete my 90-day probation to ensure I have the job, I won't have to do all these extra jobs to make ends meet. This one job will be more than enough to take care of Lexi and me and save for our home. Thank you, Lord.

January 29, 2006 — Joy & Happiness

  Father, I just want to thank you for the joy of the Lord in my life. Thank you for your happiness in my life. My joy and happiness are not found in a man or a job, but in you, Lord. Father, I just need you to encourage me in my spirit, man.

  Lord, maybe you are preparing me for something that's going to happen. I don't know, but whatever it is, help me through it. And Father, I have given it all up for the kingdom of God. Father, thank you for making me laugh, smile, and giggle again. Love you, Lord. And I bind the hands and plans of the enemy in Jesus' name.

February 15, 2006 — Orientation Dy

LORD, THANK YA!!! Today is orientation day for my new job!! Oh gosh, my pay will be doubled, and once I finish my probation period, I can stop secret shopping and spend more time with my baby girl and writing and reading. Thank you!! Today is a great day!!

February 16, 2006 — The Interview

Lord, yesterday was a great day. I went in for an interview and orientation for a job I took a test months ago. I felt so blessed and as if I was in the right place. Things are finally beginning to look up for Lexi and me. Thank you, Lord. I can't wait to start.

February 23, 2006 — A Piece of my Passion

I listened to Juanita Bynum's song, "A Piece of My Passion." It has blessed me so much. And another song called "We Wait." Father, I'll wait for you. Thank you, father, that I have given up everything for your kingdom.

February 24, 2006 — Just for Me

I went to see *Medea's Family Reunion*. There were laughter and tears. There was a young woman who's a single mom. Then there's a bus driver who's also a single dad, and he's been admiring her. They finally got together. It was so perfect. They fell in love, and in the end, they got married. In her vows, she said she could see how much God loved her. Also, she said she could see how God created her just for him. Another actress stated that God created her husband just for her.

Father, I know you have someone just for me. Father, I finally realized that you know what's best for me. Daddy, you created me, you called me, you knew everything I would go through, all the wrong choices I would make, all the sins I would commit, and all the wrong and bad relationships I would get involved in.

Daddy, you know all my likes and dislikes in men. You know what my heart desires. You know what and who will make me happy, love me, my baby, and accept Lexi as his own. You know who won't molest, abuse, or take advantage of my baby girl. Thank you, Lord.

Father, you know whom I will love, honor, submit to, and vice versa. You know who you created me to help fulfill your vision for his life and our family. You know who will help me to come into my destiny. And who will help me to share my gift of writing. Father, you know who'll love Janice and whom I will love. You know who you created just for me and me for him. You know, Father, and so I rest in that. I trust you, Lord. I leave it all up to you because I know you know me. And I thank and praise you for that. Thank you, Lord.

LORD, YOU KNOW, AND I REST IN THAT YOU KNOW. Thank you, Father. Father, now that I realize that you know, I pray that you will help me understand and receive.

Father, I don't want to make any mistakes by getting into any relationship you do not ordain. Father, help me know and rest and wait on you. LORD, I AWAIT THE OVERFLOW.

March 14, 2006 — New Job Start Day

My Father, my Lord, my God, and my King, you've been so good to Lexi and me. Over a year ago, I applied for a job with the State. I took the test in December, and I went for orientation and interview on 2/15/06. We were told that they would call that week. I confessed, and I believe on 3/7/06, as I was driving down 11th street, I said I would call to find out the progress.

Father, you reminded me of when I was in Jamaica, and my brother and I would plant peas and corn and then go back the next day to see if it grew. So, Lord, what you were saying to me is to leave it; I've already prayed, confessed, and thank you. Just leave it. So, I said, "Ok, Lord, I'm just going to leave it, and I'm not going to call." Father, I thank you because, the next day, I got a letter to do my physical, and the day after that, which was the 9th, I got a call that my start date would be Monday.

However, because I needed to give my job two weeks' notice out of respect, my new start date will be 3/20/06. Father, I thank you so much. I didn't have many casual clothes to wear, and you blessed me with some Father. I thank you so much. I'm grateful. Now, Father, I can do nothing of myself. I need you to go with me. I need you, Lord.

Thank you, Lord. I needed some money to buy some business shirts. The only money I had was my rent money of $650. I took $100, hoping the Landlord wouldn't deposit the check until I could replace it. Lord, I was in my living room praying when I realized that my new rent since we took the landlord to court is only $550, not $650. Thank you, Lord!!

March 20, 2006 — Manifestation

Today, I begin my new job! Thank you, Lord. And the pay is beautiful! Lord, all those years struggling, living in a studio apartment, and sharing a full-size bed with my baby girl for eight years, and today, I can begin to see the light at the end of the tunnel. Thank you, Lord!

March 21, 2006 — Order My Steps

Father, thank you for yesterday at my new job. God, you've been so faithful to Lexi and me. Thank you for ordering my steps to apply for this job. We spent most of the day doing paperwork, life insurances, retirement plan, etc. Thank you, Lord, that things are finally beginning to come together for Lexi and me after all these years of struggling.

Father, help me be faithful to you, stay focused, and not get involved with bad company. Help me not get distracted by the enemy, who might send males in my path to detour me. I will stay focused. I reinforce that I do not date men at my job. Thank you for blessing me with godly friends, supervisors, and please, I pray, Lord, that I will get a reasonable caseload. Thank you, Father.

April 2, 2006 — Double Pay

Father, my Lord, my daddy, I thank you so much for your goodness and your mercy. Currently, I'm in training for my new job with the State, with a beginning pay of $40,351 when I applied. I believe it was stated that we got a raise, so it's about $42000. Thank you, Lord!!!

The training is like being back in school all over again. Well, I don't mind it. I loved school, and there's a lot of information to learn. Father, I thank you for your favor with my trainers, co-workers, supervisors, and clients. I believe that I can do all things through Christ who strengthens me. This pay doubles what I was making at my last job. THANK YOU, LORD!!!

April 10, 2006 — Declare & Decree

Lord, I thank you for all that you are doing in my life this resurrection season. I praise, honor, and bless you for you and who you are to me. Lord, I speak your word, blessings over me and Lexi's life. Thank you, Father, that Lexi and I are victorious in Jesus' name. We are conquerors, and no weapon formed against us shall prosper.

All our needs are met in Jesus' name. Lexi and I are seated with Christ in heavenly places. We're joint-heirs with Christ. We walk in the fruit of the Spirit. Lexi and I are women of a quiet and gentle spirit. We are **Proverbs 31** women, in Jesus' name. I speak life and not death. My flesh is crucified, and my tongue is saved. I am a good woman, mother, wife, employee, and child of God. I am a woman of character, integrity, honor, humility, anointing. I am a mighty holy and anointed woman of God.

The word of God renews my mind. I present my body to you as a living sacrifice, holy and acceptable unto you, which is my reasonable service. I will not fall, walk, or enter into temptation. I will not be in the bondage of sin, but I will walk in the ways of the Lord all the days of my life.

I crucify my flesh and put it under subjection to the power and authority of the Holy Ghost. I am a vessel of God, meet for the master's use. Thank you, Lord, for forgiving me of my sins, faults, and shortcomings. I sever everything that has attached itself to me that is not of you. I sever soul ties, relationships, and every situation that is not of you. I plead the blood of Jesus in the name of Jesus Christ.

Father, I pray that you will release me from everything that is not like you. I send the anointing to destroy every yoke, bondage, moment, sickness, pain, molestation, and the like in Jesus' name, and I declare that I am released now in Jesus' name. Father, I thank you for cleansing and delivering me from everything that is not like you in every area of my life, and I thank you for setting me free in Jesus' name.

Lord, I retract everything I spoke over my life and Lexi's that was not your will. Every plan, hope, and dream that was not of you, I cancel them in Jesus' name. Lord, with the power and authority you've given me through the Lord and Savior Jesus Christ, I detached myself from everything and everyone that is not of your will. I render them powerless, ineffective, over, and done with. I put them all under the blood of the Lord Jesus Christ. I declare and decree that not another thought, memory, desire, or regret about my life and past. Thank you, Lord.

Now, Father, I bind the enemy and his plans in the name of Jesus Christ. I bind the enemy from attacking my thoughts, ideas, or dreams. Devil, your plans are ineffective, powerless, and of no effect in Jesus' name. You are a liar; the blood of Jesus Christ is against you. I am free in Jesus' name. I walk in the freedom and newness that Christ has set me free to walk and live in, in Jesus' name. Lord, I thank you for giving me a new heart, desire, zeal, and passion for you.

Lord, I turn my heart, sight, mind, and thoughts towards you. Loving you, Lord, getting to know you more and better. And Father, I thank you for blessing me with my God-ordained husband in due time. Thank you for aligning our paths so that he can find Lexi and me. Thank you, Lord. It is done in Jesus' name. Father, I refuse to get into any relationship that isn't ordained and God-sent. By the anointing of God, I will know if you send a man into my life or if it is the enemy.

I bind Satan from sending any man my way in Jesus' name. My husband is a God-sent. I will know he's of God, and I will not fall to the tricks and plans of the enemy in Jesus' name. Thank you for your grace and love. Thank you that I am gracefully beautiful and feminine from the inside out.

May 15, 2006 — Learning

Lord, I thank you for my new job. I am learning so much. I have met some wonderful people, my caseload is interesting, and I desire to make a difference. Thank you, Lord.

May 31, 2006 — Summer Mess-Ups

My father and Lord, Savior, my only true love, I love you, and I worship you, Lord. Father, I love you so much. I trust and admire you, Lord. You're so precious and special to me. You've been good to Lexi and me. You've been kind, gracious, and merciful to us. LORD, I ADORE YOU!!

Father, Lord, you know that my heart desires to live for you all the days of my life. As I woke up this morning, you laid on my heart that I usually mess up with guys during the summer. I would meet guys who aren't exactly what my heart desires, but they're nice, and I'll settle or compromise in what I pray and say, "Well, maybe this is the one. There are some things that I don't like about him, but maybe he's the one."

But the truth is, they're not the ones! I always end up miserable, unhappy, and have regrets, so I finally decided that I wouldn't do that anymore. Daddy, you made me, and you created me in your image. You know why I am the way I am. I feel the way I do, why I have the desires I do, why I desire the man of God that I do, and why I don't want a man that I must help to build. Please help me to perfect my husband's list and help me not compromise for what my heart desires.

You, my Lord, have put those desires in me; however, Lord, take out every desire, want, and need in me that is not like you. I don't want to miss the blessing you have for me. Lord, thank you for dropping in my spirit that *"In the 7th month, you are going to bless me in the area of my relationship and my husband."* So, Lord, I await.

June 1, 2006 — No More Distractions

There's a guy that works at my job. He's very fond of me, and he invited me to attend church with him. It didn't work out, so we talked on the phone for a few hours. But I know that he's not the one for me. Plus, I don't date guys that I work with. Therefore, it's my duty not to get distracted by him and stay focused. This seems to happen every few years. It looks as if I continue to meet guys that are not the one, but because of church folks, instead of walking away, I'll give them a chance and waste time like the Children of Israel. Well, not this year and not anymore.

I'm waiting on you this time, Lord. I refuse to settle, and I'll stay by myself before I settle. Father, I mean to live and do right despite me. Please bless me and help me stay focused in every area of my life. Father, I submit to you totally in every area of my life, in Jesus' name. I love you, Lord.

July 4, 2006 — Honor God with My Cookies

Thank you for this day off. As I sit at my computer and allow you to lead and direct my fingers, heart, mind, and thoughts, you gave me this book about "Cookies." You want me to wait for you to bless me with my husband.

I will honor you in my body, and I need to make up in my mind that I will wait for you to manifest my husband, no other way. It's your way or no way. Thank you, Lord. I will be writing soon.

July 16, 2006 — Daddy Dearest

Daddy dearest, thank you for your love, grace, mercy, forgiveness, and righteousness. Thank you for watching over Lexi and me and keeping us. Thank you for the revelation that you are my DADDY DEAREST. Daddy, you love me so much that you gave your only begotten son for me. Abba, you are so sweet, kind, loving, and full of tender mercies.

Lord, you've been so good to me. You've supplied every need. You know my heart's desire. You know that your will is my desire. And I know that you are my daddy, dearest. That's all that matters. Love you, Father.

July 22, 2006 — Bless Me Indeed

Hello, Father, my daddy dearest. How are you doing today? I bless and praise your holy name. I thank you for today - a day of rest and relaxation for me. Six months ago, you laid on my heart that you would bless me in July, this month, with my husband. Several guys were interested in taking me out, but I declined because I know they're not the ones.

And Lord, here I am waiting to receive my blessing from you, despite me. I'm expecting daily for you to bless me and enlarge my territory. I pray, Daddy, that you will keep back every counterfeit the enemy would send my way. Confuse them and keep them away from me. I will do your will, oh Lord, as I wait patiently for you. Thank you, Lord.

Father, today as I took a nap, I dreamt about Mary and Martha and Lazarus's story. In the dream, I heard these words: *"second chances."* Father, what does that mean? What are you talking about? Thank you for the revelation and insight.

August 2, 2006 — Sister to Sister

I had "Sister to Sister" at church, and it was such a blessing. I was blessed to minister about "An Exchanged Life" **Galatians 2:17-21 and Isiah 40:28-32.** Four other sisters ministered, and then we had Q &A. Father, so much came out of this time. Women who are saved, sanctified, filled with the Holy Ghost, and love the Lord, but we have many issues to deal with.

Sisters were dealing with low self-esteem, fornication, masturbation, lesbianism, wanting to get married, getting out of a marriage, etc. Father, even though we love you, at times, we mess up, slip and fall, but thanks be to you, Lord, you give us the strength to get back up again.

Father, you gave me so much love and compassion for my sisters and me. And I know that you delivered me that night. There wasn't any yelling or screaming. I know that there was a breakthrough, healing, and deliverance within me. And I know you did the same for my sisters in attendance. Thank you, Lord.

August 4, 2006 — Feeling Horny

Father, last night as I laid down, I thought about being married and intimate, about being with my husband. Yes, Lord, I desire to be married for several reasons, and intimacy is one of them. I was somewhat horny, and I just began to praise you and lift my hands, and you brought me to **Philippians 4:19, My God shall supply all of my needs according to his riches in glory.**

Father, I thank you for that. You know that intimacy with my husband is a need, and you said that you would supply that need. This morning, as I woke up, you said: *"receive it."* So, I receive every blessing you have for me in Jesus' name. Thank you for supplying every need in Jesus' name.

Lord, as I got up and sat at my desk, looking through my window, I heard the word *"deliverance."* Deliverance Ministry. Thank you, Lord, for a deliverance ministry.

August 6, 2006 — Lexi's Birthday

Father, today is my baby girl's birthday!! Oh, I am so grateful for her. Lord, you sure have brought us a mighty long way. You have blessed her and kept her and granted her favor wherever she goes. I pray for your continual blessings over Lexi. The best thing I can do for her is to live a pleasing life before you and her and pray for her. Thank you for the grace and wisdom to live for you for her.

Thank you for keeping her and enlarging her territory. Thank you that Lexi is blessed going, blessed coming, blessed in the city and the fields. I pray the Daniel blessing over Lexi. Lord, give her wisdom, knowledge, understanding. Make her wise in her life and the decisions that she will make. Help her honor you in her mind, soul, body, and spirit.

I pray manifestation of your healing in her from the crown of her head to the very soles of her feet. I pray for Alexia's cognition. I bind learning disability, and I pray for a release in her in Jesus' name. I curse, rebuke generation curses, and I speak fourth-generation blessings and healings. I curse and rebuke learning disability out of my family and bloodline.

I rebuke learning disability, cognitive impairment, and developmental disability out of Lexi. And I command your total healing to manifest in Jesus' name. I declare and decree that not another child in my bloodline will be affected by a learning disability or any kind of sickness, disease, or developmental disability.

I plead the blood even over those things that I don't know in her bloodline from her father's side. But, Lord, you know, and I take authority in Jesus' name. I speak the uncommon blessing over, in, and through Lexi in Jesus' name.

Father, may you perfect Lexi's heart towards you, and may she live for you all the days of her life. I pray that Alexia is godly, respectful, obedient and that she will live for you forever! I declare and decree that Lexi will never depart from you, your ways, or your words, but for the rest of her life, Lord, she will live for you only. I pray that Lexi will keep her eyes, heart, mind, and soul focused on you forever.

Thank you for blessing Lexi with godly friends and teachers. Thank you for making a way out of no way. Thank you for supplying all Alexia's needs, and I thank you that Alexia has everything she needs. No weapon that is formed against her shall prosper.

Father, keep her in the palm of your hand, oh Lord, and nothing or no one can pluck her out. Thank you, Lord. I call it done in Jesus' name. Give Lexi your continual peace, guidance, healing, and grace manifestations. I speak a supernatural blessing over and in Alexia's life in Jesus' name. Good will come to Lexi always.

August 12, 2006 — A Vision

I had a vision last night. Thank you, Lord, for showing me things to come. I saw something like a stadium, but it was a church. There were thousands of people there. Then you showed me the shape of it, which was like a ship, and there were thousands of cars parked all around it. Thank you, Lord, for the revelation.

August 13, 2006 — Learning to Hear

Daddy dearest, I bless your holy name. You're worthy to be praised, worthy of all the glory and honor. At the beginning of the year, Father spoke to me and said, you would do something for me where my husband is concerned. I thought you said you would send him this year. Well, it's August, and nothing yet. But Lord, whoever it is or if I heard you right, I trust you to bring your word to pass.

I trust you because you are my daddy, dearest. I know that you have my best interests at heart, and you said you would give me the desires of my heart according to your will. So, I call it done, and I receive my Boaz in Jesus' name.

August 14, 2006 — My Father Said

A few years ago, my father in the faith, Pastor Bradshaw, gave me this theme and requested that I write it down. It was, "He was what I wanted, but he was who I needed."

Father, in Jesus' name, I need you. I confess every sin before you. Please forgive me and wash me and cleanse me from all my sin and shame in Jesus' name. Thank you for blessing me in abundance, grace, and favor. Please watch over Lexi and me and keep us safe from all harm and danger in Jesus' name.

August 17, 2006 — You are God

Lord, I went to Abundant Life in New Brunswick. Worship was awesome, and there was this song, "You are God, and you alone are God, and I worship you; you are God alone." Father, the tears just streamed down my face. I cried through worship while worshipping you. You ministered to me. And you said, *"He will find you. You don't have to do anything, go anywhere. He will find you."* You brought back the story about Rebecca, how Abraham's servant went and found her for Isaac. As I read the scripture, the servant prayed in **Genesis 24.**

Father, before Eleazar could finish those words, Rebecca came to the well. Daddy, you also brought back Ruth to me and how she was in the field gleaning, and you showed her favor in Boaz's sight. And oh, beautiful and young Esther, you also brought her back to my memory. Esther found favor in everyone's sight. And when she went to the King, he loved her, and she obtained grace and favor with him, and he made her his queen.

Lord, the same way you blessed these women, I believe, is the way that I know you've already blessed me with my husband. They were doing what they were supposed to be doing. You directed their path to be in the right place at the right time. Father, help me continue doing what you've appointed me to do, be a mother and an active member in my local church. Direct my path so that I can be in the right place at the right time to have my Boaz appointment.

Father, I thank you for anointing me to write books to bless your people. I thank you for directing my path and my husband's path for him to find me in Jesus' name. The same way you blessed me with a wonderful Church, the job I always desired, is the way you've already blessed me with my husband, and I thank you.

You have a destiny and plan for me and Alexia's life. Thank you for helping us to come into the plans and destiny you have for us. Thank you for my man of God, my husband. And I thank you for letting me know that he must fit into the vision that you've given me for my life. Lord, you are my daddy, dearest. You created me. You know me and know what I need and want.

You know who can love Lexi and accept her as his own, love her, and be a father and a daddy. You know who can love me and be my friend, husband, and lover, whom we can both love, honor, submit to and respect each other. You know, Lord, and I thank you for that in Jesus' name.

August 25, 2006 — Disney World

Abba Father, it's Friday at 8:30 a.m. sitting on flight 0000 to West Palm Beach, Florida. Lexi and I are on our way to Port St Luci to visit my biological father and take her to Disney World for her birthday. It's such a blessing to be able to go on vacation. My daddy paid for the plane tickets, and I'm paying for our hotel and access to the park.

Thank you for blessing us to be able to travel. I pray, Lord, that you watch over us and protect us and keep us safe from all harm and danger. Thank you for the guardian angels you've given charge over us to keep us in all our ways. Thank you, Lord and father, for blessing me with my husband this week. Thank you for my Boaz appointment.

September 2, 2006 — A Sensitive Ear & Heart

Abba Father, we're on our way back from Disney to Port St Luci so we can prepare for our trip back home on 9/3/06. So much has happened, and I thank you for helping me to be more sensitive to you. When I got here last Friday, you impressed on my heart that someone was in my apartment back home using my internet. I called my phone, and it was busy.

All week when I called my phone, it was busy. Then there were times it would ring, and at other times, it would be busy. Eventually, I called Netscape on September 1 and learned that my internet service had been used all week, and it was currently being used.

I called the police, and they went there and arrested Ryan. (Note: Ryan is the stepson of my very good friend and neighbor, who I've known since he was a kid.) I'm so disappointed that he would do that. I've been good to him. He's been like a little brother to me. He could have asked me, and I would have let him use my internet when I wasn't home. How foolish of him!! I told the cops I did not want to press charges, but they said they have to arrest him since they caught him there. So sad!!!

Nevertheless, Holy Spirit, I thank you for revealing the secret thing to me. Father, I leave it in your hands, and I thank you for working everything out for Ryan. Thank you for your guidance and your protection. I bless your holy name.

October 1, 2006 — Talk to Yourself

Father, I began to feel down as I usually feel around my birthday. Feelings of not accomplishing much and being unhappy with many things and events in my life. Last year I decided that I would not allow the enemy to attack me and cause me to feel down on my birthday.

So not this year, devil, or ever again, will I feel down on my birthday. The Holy Spirit reminded me of David's story, how he encouraged himself in the Lord. Every day, Lord, you have been bringing back that scripture to me, and I thank you for that.

As David in **Psalm 103** spoke to himself and encouraged himself in you, so I speak to myself. Janice, you are loved, anointed, gifted, and the favor of God is upon your life. Janice, God has been good to you. He's kept you and brought you from a mighty long way.

Janice, Christ, has made you whole, healed, delivered, and destined you. You have a call upon your life. Janice, God has already blessed you with your husband. Believe in God for the manifestation in Jesus' name.

Janice, you are a great mother. You have much to teach Alexia. Janice, I speak the uncommon blessings over your life. I speak the Daniel blessings over your life. I speak the manifestation of everything you've been praying for. You are blessed, loved, protected. Something good is going to happen to you today. Money is looking for you to bless you. All your needs are met according to God's riches in glory through Christ Jesus. Janice, you have everything you need.

October 5, 2006 — God Has Worked It Out

Father, I had a dream. I was telling someone that Alexia is going to make it. God has already worked it out, and all is well in her life.

October 11, 2006 — Day of Reflection

Father, today I celebrate my 29th birthday! It was a wonderful and blessed day. I had offers to go out for dinner dates, but I turned them down. I don't want to share my birthday with just any guy. I began my day with prayer, dropped Lexi off, came home, showered, took a nap, woke up, worked on my book *Praying for Our Children* for a while, took another nap, and worked on my book again. I bought myself some hair and went to dinner with Lexi, Prophetess Jackson, and sister Hodge at Red Lobster.

I got calls and cards from my co-workers, lots of hugs and kisses, and I love you from Lexi. I love her so much. She's the sweetest thing!! As I awoke this morning, you gave me **Philippians 4:19 But my God shall supply all your need according to his riches in glory by Christ Jesus**.
And Father, my needs are as follows:
1. Total deliverance and healing for Alexia
2. My husband's manifestation, helping us to meet, coming together, and getting married.
3. Bless the coming together of me, Lexia, and my husband.

You said, when we pray, believe we've received, and I believe that I have received my husband. You said for me to ask, and it shall be given. I have asked, and I believe that I have received. Thank you for your healing, power, blessings, provisions, favor. Thank you for making room for my gifts and Alexia. Thank you that my husband is a gift. Thank you for our home(house), businesses, and my books' publication and multi-million sales.

Thank you for sending me the publication company, Information, and thank you for my ministry's exposure, for opening doors, and closing the doors the enemy has opened in Jesus' name. Thank you, Lord, and I bless your holy name.

At dinner, Prophetess gave me this scripture from the Holy Spirit. **Jeremiah 29:11, For I know the thoughts that I think toward you, saith the Lord, thoughts of peace, and not of evil, to give you an expected end.**

Thank you, Father, for your word.

Moments of Gratitude

November 15, 2006   *Speak What You Want*

Father, thank you for these last few weeks. As I begin to think things over, I see how blessed Lexi and I are. You've been faithful and supplied all our needs to pay our bills. I didn't go to the supermarket this week, but we have everything we need. I didn't fill the gas tank up this week, but you allowed the gas from last week to sustain us through this week.

This morning, I dropped Lexi off and came home to do a little praying and reading before work, and as I moved my devotional book, I found $15. Thank you so much, Lord. I appreciate it. Father, I love my job. This is the job I always wanted, except for writing full time. Thank you for your favor with all I work with, my supervisor, and all those in management.

This temporary supervisor is attempting to make my job miserable. She's extremely anal and picky, but Father, I take authority over that spirit of torment in Jesus' name. I am thankful for this job that provides very well for Lexi and me, and I refuse to be miserable because of a spirit of torment in my supervisor.

I release a spirit of peace and freedom. As I think back when the administrator moved me from one unit to another, I was upset because I had set my things up, and I liked that unit. Then I had to move my items and start over. Now I thank you for moving me out of that unit, and I thank you that I don't have that supervisor anymore. Thank you for working it out, Father.

I pray for our new supervisor that we'll be getting. I pray that he/she is good, kind, understanding, helpful, easy to talk to, not anal or picky, works with us, and is preferably born again. And Holy Spirit, add anything else you need to add.

November 20, 2006 — I Want a Rich Husband

Father, I thank you for helping me to be disciplined in my finances. Thank you that I am a tither, and I give offerings. Thank you for increasing Lexi and me. I remember, a few months ago, while at the copier, the Holy Spirit said, *"You're praying for a rich husband."* So, Lord, help me to maintain my finances and keep them in order. Help me, Lord, to do right and continue to bring my tithes and offering, pay my rent and bills on time, and just do right. Thank you, Lord.

November 24, 2006 — Thankful

Father, yesterday was Thanksgiving Day. I have so much to be thankful for. I thank you for the Godhead. You have been so good to Alexia and me. You've been faithful, and you've never left us or forsaken us, and for that, I thank you. Thank you that I have never depended on anyone else for anything. Lexi and I can walk, talk, and see. We can hear, dress, and feed ourselves. Thank you that we go to sleep, and you wake us up.

I have tremendous joy. We have food, family, and friends. I have my books and my music. You've anointed me to study, read, write, teach, preach, prophesy, lay hands, and pray. Sing, dance, clap my hands, play musical instruments. I can go into the Bible and get a word from glory. Thank you, Lord.

Thank you for blessing Lori and Althea and their husbands with their babies. I thank you that all is well with Alexia and that she can do for herself, take care of herself, and make the right decisions. Thank you for your peace and that the situation has been turned around, and I thank you that the curse has been canceled.

I thank you that Jesus took every curse upon him, and Lexi has been delivered from generational curses and learning disability. And Father, I thank you for my husband. I declare and decree that he is a mighty man of God you made, especially for me, and me especially for him. Thank you that he will love Lexi and take her as his own, and we will love each other in Jesus' name, Amen.

November 25, 2006 — Not God's Will

Well, Daddy, I'm happy to say that I let this person go because I knew he wasn't my husband. I think I wanted him to be, but I knew that he was not who you have for me. I thank you for the strength to do so. Thank you for helping me to be able to see with the eyes of an eagle and giving me the wisdom to ask the right questions.

Those were my emotions working with the enemy so that I could miss my destiny. I thank you. I know and believe that you have a mighty man of valor for Lexi and me, and I thank you for him, and I wait patiently in expectation for him. Thank you, Lord.

December 1, 2006 — Endless Thanksgiving

Lord, thank you for the new things you're doing in Alexia's life. I thank you for blessing Lori and Althea with babies. Thank you in advance for my husband, for blessing, my ministry, and my books, for opening doors for me to teach and preach your Word, and for prophesying.

Thank you for anointing me. Thank you for my new job, Father! My list is endless. Every day, I will give you thanks and express my gratitude.

December 30, 2006 — God, You Are Credible

Father, how I thank and praise your name for bringing Alexia and me to the end of another year. As I woke this morning, I heard these words, "*Lord, you are credible.*" Credible means capable of being believed, worthy of confidence, reliable. Lord, you have good credit with Lexi and me. You've been so good to us. I think about the song, "When I look back over my life and think things over."

God, you've been so good. This week, I was thinking about when I graduated from Rutgers and applied for a job at the Association paying $30K. I didn't get it, but there was one paying $17,992 available. I took that because Alexia and I needed to eat. Then I got promoted and should have been getting one pay but got less. But despite all that, I was thankful, did my job with joy, paid my tithes, and then you blessed me with a job paying over $40k, starting 3/06. Lord, thank you!

I remember I wanted a church home, and I went to St Paul's in July of 7/05. I went to ask about summer camp for Lexi on a Tuesday night, and I haven't stopped going. You've shown me favor there. I'm so happy about a new church home. Lord, I thank you.

When I look at Alexia and see how far you've brought her, Father, I thank you. And Lord, I've been praying and believing you for my husband, and I know, according to **Mark 11:24,** what things I desire when I pray, believe that I have received them, and I shall have them.

Father, you've blessed Alexia and me with my new job, and you've blessed us with a church home that I'm happy about, and Father, I know that you've blessed me with my husband. I thank you for him and everything you've done and will do. Thank you, Lord.

December 31, 2006 — A Blessed Year

Lord, this year has been an amazing though, though there were some tough times. I started a new job, met new people, and Alexia and I are doing wonderfully. Thank you, Lord!

January 1, 2007 — A New Year

Father, as I sat in church this New Year's Eve, I couldn't contain the tears that ran down my cheeks. Lord, you've been so good to Lexi and me. And I thank you for your goodness and mercy.

I wish my husband were sitting next to me, but I know you will manifest him in due time. Thank you, father, for sparing our lives to see a brand-new year. I speak greater heights, deeper depths in you, Lord.

January 7, 2007 — To Thine Own Self be True

Father, while parts of 2006 were amazing, it was also a trying year. But we made it, and I thank you. You brought Lexi and me in and out as you promised in your word. And as I look forward to 2007, it is a year that I want to work on me. I desire to be a better woman, mother, and wife. Thank you, Lord.

January 16, 2007 — Destiny's Path

Thank you for speaking *"Destiny's Path"* into my spirit. Life and this walk with the Lord are like a ship on the seas. Sometimes it's windy, and the ship is tossed to and fro. Sometimes, there's peace, and the ship sails smoothly. Whatever the circumstances, that ship must get to its destination.

The song *"Your Steps Have Been Ordered by The Lord"* by Fred Hammond, my favorite gospel artist. Straight and narrow is the path.

You laid on my heart, **Matthew 7:7 Ask, and it shall be given you; seek, and ye shall find; knock, and it shall be opened unto you.**

And **Matthew 7:13-14 Enter ye in at the strait gate: for wide is the gate, and broad is the way, that leadeth to destruction, and many there be which go in thereat:[14] Because strait is the gate, and narrow is the way, which leadeth unto life, and few there be that find it.**

Thank you, Father, for helping me to get on Destiny's Path. You have a plan for me and Lexi's life; therefore, we will walk in the ways of the Lord always. Today, I make up my mind to do everything God's way.

January 20, 2007 — God Has a Plan for Me

Jeremiah 29:11 For I know the thoughts that I think toward you, saith the Lord, thoughts of peace, and not of evil, to give you an expected end. Thank you for reminding me, Father.

January 16, 2007 — God's Word

As I awoke this morning at about 4:28 a.m., I heard the word: *"Finances."* Holy Spirit, what are you saying about finances? Father, I thank you for helping me see and realize that I need to spend more time reading and meditating on your Word.

Also, I need to pray, fast more, and speak your Word more. Thanks to your Word, my tongue is more disciplined and safer. Holy Spirit, I give my tongue to you. I trust you will use it as you will in Jesus' name. You've spoken so many words over me and Lexi's life.

Father, you have given me so many dreams and visions and prophetic words. Give me the strength to study and meditate on each of them. Please help me to wait patiently for you to bring them to pass and be submitted and obedient to you through it all. And Lord, I pray for Alexia's total healing. Manifestation your healing power now.

February 18, 2007 — Less Than

Preparing breakfast, thinking about a sister in the Lord, dating a man of another religious persuasion who doesn't believe that Jesus is the son of God. The Lord spoke to me and said, *"As long as you will settle for less than, then you will always get less than."*

February 19, 2007 — Meekness

As I dozed off, I saw a Bible open and the word *Meekness* in the top right-hand corner, and a hand was highlighting it. I heard or saw **John 2**. Thank you, Father. As I woke up from a dream, I could see a note with a phrase on it, but the only word I could remember is *Lack*.

Not sure what that means, but Father, I bind lack in me and Lexi's life. I speak prosperity, more than enough, pressed down, shaken together, and running over. And Father, as Moses said that he was a meek man, I speak meekness over me and Lexi's life in Jesus' name.

Moments of Gratitude

February 21, 2007 *Perplexed*

My Father, so much has been going on! My mother is here visiting, unannounced after she left about two years ago and hadn't spoken to me since and refused to talk with me because of that argument we had back then. (See my book *Praying for Our Children*.)

Sister Jackson knew and didn't tell me since my mom stayed at one of her friends' houses. I've been frustrated with my life, being tried and tested at work, but during the storms, you are still God, and I thank you for the peace that surpasses all understanding. Thank you, Lord, and I bless your Holy Name!

April 15, 2007 — Bless Your Enemies

Experiencing some attacks on my job, but while praying, the spirit of the Lord said, *"Pray for and bless your enemies, and what I said in my word, I will bring it to pass concerning your enemies."* Lord, thank you that you said: "I WILL EXALT YOU HIGH ABOVE YOUR ENEMIES." Thank you, Jesus.

April 28, 2007 — Engulf with All of God

Taking a rest in Alexia's room, and as I awoke, Holy Spirit said, *"Be engulfed with all of God."*

April 29, 2007 — Write, Writer

Holy Spirit said, *"You shall write many books, and they will bring healing and deliverance to the people."* Thank you, Lord.

July 1, 2007 — A Week in the Word

So thankful for this trip to Colorado Springs to see Andrew Womack. A much-needed trip and time to get away and spend some time in the presence of the Lord.

July 27, 2007 — Tell Your Story

As I awoke, the Holy Spirit said, *"Tell them your story."* Thank you, Jesus, for your word of encouragement to share my testimony with the world.

July 29, 2007 — Word of Wisdom

The spirit of the Lord spoke and said, *"Begin to put your messages on CDs."* Father, thank you for this word of wisdom. Thank you that you've blessed me with the people to help me in ministry. Thank you, Lord.

March 20, 2008 — *Moments of Gratitude*

This is the beginning of *Moments of Gratitude* (MOG). Thank you, Lord!

March 20, 2008 — *Pathway to No Compromise*

Today, I went to the Federal Building, and I had to go through security. I put my pocketbook through the scanner with it open, and afterward, I didn't check to make sure nothing fell out. As I returned home, I checked my bag for my disc, which contains my book, *Praying for Our Children*, and some other books, sermons, papers, articles, etc.

As I began to panic, I could hear the Holy Spirit saying, "*Don't panic. Go back to the Federal Building.*" For a moment, I was upset, and my mind began to flood with thoughts. I returned to the Federal Building and asked if they had found anything. The security said yes, but they had to check it first.

The funny thing was that, earlier, when I was at the gas station, the Lord lay on my heart, "*Pathway to no compromise,*" which means, when circumstances arise, I need to rest in the Word and not allow any doubt or compromise to take over my thoughts.

Father, I know that you love me. I refuse to entertain the lie that you allowed this to happen because you don't love me and that someone will steal my book and publish it. Lord, thank you that I quickly rebuked those thoughts and praised you. And confirmed my trust in you and thanked you for my success in advance.

March 27, 2008 — Pray for Your Enemies

Today was my day off from work, and what a beautiful day it was! I dropped off Lexi at the program and came home and spent time with Father. I've been pouring my heart out and praying for an old friend that hurt me.

Initially, Father, you told me to pray, and I did, but there was no heart. So, I prayed and asked you to touch my heart to pray passionately for him. Father, you touched my heart, and I could cry out for him as I could cry out for Lexi many times. Thank you, Lord.

March 28, 2008 — Favor

Today at work, we celebrated Women's Month. We had a beautiful program, lunch was delicious, and everything seemed perfect. We had a guest, and I was blessed to be the one to interview her. I studied and prayed as I desire to do everything with excellence.

When the time came for the interview, I had memorized the questions while gazing at them periodically. Everyone was amazed at my approach when it was done, and I was shocked that I hadn't done it before.

When my union rep asked me, I declined, but then she insisted. When I asked why she thought I should do it, she stated that I was energetic and friendly. A few days later, I accepted. You see, I've been at this job for two years. My first year was challenging, and she had to intervene between me and my supervisor, who, for some reason, seemed to have it in for me.

She also had to step in with those in managerial positions, and I was so happy that they were there to see me in another light, one of whom praised me. Then I was pleased that I accepted. Thank you, Lord, as I can do nothing of myself. Thank you for the favor!

March 29, 2008 — Love

Today is Saturday, and I had to work, but I would have preferred to be home in bed. On Saturdays, I usually get up early for my devotional then go back to bed. But Father, I thank you that I have a job.

After work, Lexi and I went to a movie, went shopping, and had dinner. We talked, laughed, hugged, kissed, and came home and enjoyed the rest of the evening together. Lord, I thank you!

April 1, 2008 — Laughter & Psalm 23 Husband

Today was a tough day at work. It was rainy, and I was dragging all day. My whole day was rough, but I had to quickly cast every care and burden on the Lord. I began to look for something to give God thanks for. So, I thought about my friends and how we could talk, eat, and laugh.

Even though we always eat and laugh at lunchtime, I don't think I have ever given thanks for being able to have lunch and laugh with my friends. Thank you, Lord!

When I picked up Lexi, she had her school pictures. They are beautiful, and they put a smile on my face. Lexi and I talked and laughed all the way home. Later, we went to Bible studies, and the study was on **Psalm 23**, talking about The Good Shepherd.

It's ironic because I thought that I need to write something on **Psalm 23** about my husband and how I want a **Psalm 23** Husband. Thank you, Lord.

Janice Hylton Thompson

October 17, 2008 — Remember When?

I've been feeling discouraged lately. I need to take some time to stay in the presence of the Lord. Did I have faith at all? I need to retrace the beginning of my faith walk. What happened? Thank you, Lord, for bringing me out and through.

November 25, 2008 — Who Changed?

Did God change? Did you change? God changes not; He is the same yesterday, today, and forever. So, the common denominator here is me. I need to get my eyes back on Jesus, who is both the author and finisher of my faith. Thank you, Lord!

November 26, 2008 — Start with Thanksgiving

I woke up today with this thought in my heart: "*Start with thanksgiving!*" God knows exactly what I needed this morning, and so I will begin my day by giving thanks for those things I take for granted.

Thank you, Lord, that I can get up out of bed, walk, brush my teeth, wash, dress, and feed myself. Lord, I thank you for those little things I often overlook. Thank you, Lord!

November 30, 2008 — Do the Right Thing!

Sometimes, you must check yourself and tell yourself to *"Do the Right Thing!"* My father in the faith Pastor Marvin Bradshaw, Sr, often said, "it might not feel good to do the right thing, but it is always right to do the right thing. So, thank you, Lord.

December 2, 2008 — Agreeing with God

The most extraordinary and beautiful thing about the Holy Spirit is that He ministers to us. Sometimes we wrestle within ourselves, and we don't even know what we're fighting against, but He knows.

And, at times, the Holy Spirit ministers to us in simple little phrases that, when we think about it, we can't help but say Amen! And so, He says, *"Agree with God!"* Thank you, Lord.

December 3, 2008 — Pray for Alexia

We are all intercessors, as we are commissioned to pray for one another. And so today, the Holy Spirit said to me, *"Pray for Alexia. God will perfect that which concerns her."* Now, I know that I will pray for Alexia even if I don't pray for anyone else.

But apparently, the Holy Spirit knows best, and He wants me to pray even more for my baby girl. The ironic thing is that I am currently working on a book titled *Praying for Our Children*.

December 18, 2008 — Small Beginnings

I haven't been able to find a place to have my Bible Studies. So, I decided to have it at my house, and I am so blessed! Thank you, Lord.

December 31, 2008 — Reason to Praise the Lord

The end of an old year and stepping into a new one! I've got a reason to praise the Lord. I'm alive and well! Alexi and I are healthy; we have food, clothing, shelter, and I have a job. We are not in the hospital because we are healthy. We have the activity of our limbs.

Therefore, admittedly, I've got a reason to praise the Lord. I adore you, Jesus, and I thank you!

January 1, 2009 — Fruitfulness

The number 9 means fruitfulness, harvest, and abundance. Lord, thank you for a new day and a new year. Father, you said death and life are in the power of the tongue.

Therefore, I speak life, blessing, harvest, fruitfulness, and abundance in Lexi's and my life. 2009 will be a year of reaping and harvest for Lexi and me. This year will be one of manifested blessings and prosperity. Thank you, Lord.

February 12, 2009 — She's the One

Today I went to the laundry, and I had $5.00 leftover that I thought I put in my pocket. I came home and was going back to the laundry to put the clothes in the dryer. I checked to see if I had the $5.00, and I couldn't find it. I searched for my wallet, coat, etc., and I didn't find it.

So, I got some change that I had at the house. I was distraught because I believe that I shouldn't lose any money. I'm a tither; I support other ministries, and I'm a giver. I don't care if it's $5 or 5 cents. I shouldn't lose any money! Didn't God say he would rebuke the canker and palmerworm?

Finally, I decided to go back to the laundromat, and an older man who was seated there pointed to me and said, "She's the one." The laundry attendant handed me the $5.00. I was ecstatic. This truly kind older gentleman said, "I saw her when she put those clothes in there. That's her money!" Thank you, Jesus!

February 13, 2009 — Tiny Blessings

I was looking for the computer speakers' plug for about three days, but I couldn't find it anywhere. Alexia was finishing her dinner when she asked, "Mommy, what are you looking for? Do you need help?" That touched my heart. Thank you, Lord!

September 23, 2009 — Favor

Today, I got pulled over because of a "supposedly" broken headlight. The cop asked if I knew my headlight was out, and I said, "No, I just got it fixed." He said, "Well, it's not working." I then said, "Well, please don't give me a ticket because I already got one last month for the same thing!" He then said, "Well, maybe you have a shortage, and you need to get it checked out."

Thank you, Lord, that I didn't get a ticket!

November 1, 2010 — Your Husband is Held up

I wanted to add my testimony of how the Lord spoke to me about my husband. Of course, I have a dating journal coming soon, so please be sure to look out for that. But, I wanted to share my testimony here to encourage you to continue to pray and be open to the leading of the Lord.

One day in early November 2010, I was going to the bank. The day was seasonable, overcast, cloudy, and bleak. As I was almost to my bank, Holy Spirit said, *"Look Up."* When I looked up, the sky looked like there would be a storm. The clouds looked black and stormy. Holy Spirit said, *"your husband has been held up. Some women have laid claims to him as theirs, but they are not their husbands. You need to pray that your husband is released."*

Right there and then, I prayed something like: "Father in the name of the Lord Jesus Christ, I thank you for giving me this revelation. I thank you for blessing me with my husband. I thank you that you answered my prayers the first time I prayed. I thank you for hearing and blessing me with the desires of my heart.

Now, father, thank you for the power and authority you gave me according to **Luke 10:19** that says **Behold, I give unto you power to tread on serpents and scorpions, and over all the power of the enemy: and nothing shall by any means hurt you.**

Abba father, with the power and authority you gave me through the Lord Jesus Christ, I bind the hands of the devil. Devil, I rebuke you in Jesus' name. You are a defeated foe. You are under my feet. You have no power and authority over my life. Satan, I render you ineffective and inoperative in Jesus' name. You demon from the pits of hell, I command you to take your dirty, filthy hands off my husband.

You spirit of deception, confusion, and destruction that comes to kill, steal, and destroy, I bind you in the name of Jesus. I command you to release my husband now, in Jesus' name. Lose your hold in Jesus' name. I command you to go back to the pit from whence you came in Jesus' name. I bind you and all demonic forces that are keeping my husband and me apart in the name of Jesus. I command you to let my husband go now, in Jesus' name!!

In the name of Jesus, Father, I thank you that my husband has been released in Jesus' name. I thank you that our paths will cross, and he will find me. I pray that I will hear from you about who he is. Thank you that my husband matches my husband's list and is a confirmation. I thank you that my father in the faith will also confirm that he is the one in Jesus' name.

And father, I pray for the ladies laying claims to my husband. I pray that you will speak to them and reveal your plan for them and their lives in Jesus' name. I pray that you will bless them all with husbands in Jesus' name.

Father, I thank you again for my husband; I thank you that he will find me. I thank you that we will meet in due time, in Jesus' name. And Lord, I thank you, and I receive my wonderful husband now in Jesus name." Hallilujah, thank Ya Lord!

I met my husband the following year, on November 4th, 2011.

Janice Hylton Thompson

December 25, 2010   A Moment in Time

Up early this Christmas morning and getting ready to take my flight to Shreveport, Louisiana, to visit my godmother. As I gathered the last of my things, I began to look for a little book called *The Gift of Wisdom for Mothers*.

Finally, I found it and placed it in my computer bag. Then the Spirit of the Lord spoke quietly to my heart and said, *"Everyday begin to meditate on scriptures about being a mother."*

You see, I've been having some challenges within myself this year when I realized that I must take care of her for the rest of my and Lexi's life. I must tell her the things she needs to do.

As a parent, when you have a child, you know that, eventually, they will be able to take care of themselves and live on their own. But, for a single moment, it hit me that I must do things for Lexi for the rest of our lives, even though God has given me promises from his word about her.

Therefore, I put all my faith and trust in God that He will bring His Word to pass in Jesus' name. Thank you, Lord, for giving me wisdom on how to meditate on your promises in every area of my life.

I pray for other parents of special needs children in Jesus' name. Please give us all the grace and strength we need to take care of our babies.

March 25, 2011 — No Whipped Cream

People who know me know that I love a Dunkaccino from Dunkin' Donuts! I go to Dunkin' Donuts a few times each week and order a large Dunkaccino with whipped cream. Sometimes, I wouldn't get the whipped cream because I'd think to myself, "I'm helping my health." (LOL!!) Of course, that didn't work because the next time I went to Dunkin' Donuts, I ordered my regular with whipped cream.

This morning I went to Dunkin' Donuts, and would you believe they didn't have any whipped cream? So off to the next store I went, and guess what? That store and two other Dunkin' Donuts were all out of whipped cream. I think the Lord is playing tricks on me.

April 18, 2011 — Magnify the Lord

Today was a day of despair. As I was up and about, there was a simple voice that said, *"Magnify the Lord, rehearse what God has done for you, stay full of God."* Holy Spirit, I thank you for ministering to me in my time of despair of how to praise my way out of any pit! Amen.

April 22, 2011 — Restful Weekend

I had the most restful weekend ever. I stayed in bed all day Friday and most of Saturday! Thank you, Lord, for such a wonderful weekend of rest.

June 5, 2011 — *Hiding under a Rock*

Have you ever had a day that you wanted to hide under a rock? Today was one of those days for me. And as I thought about it, I thought of Jesus as my rock. So, Lord, thank you that you are my Solid Rock!!

June 28, 2011 — *Fender Bender Almost*

This afternoon, I turned on 18th Avenue and felt the need to start praying. When I got to the red light, there was a car in front of me. My foot was on the brakes while I was looking at some of the new houses that were recently built.

To my surprise, my car was still moving slowly! But thankfully, I looked up just in time to step harder on my brakes and prevent what could have been a fender bender. Thank you, Lord.

July 7, 2011 — *Turn Here*

I was driving to work along my usual route. As I got to Clinton Avenue, the Holy Spirit said to me, *"Turn here!"* I was a little skeptical because I'm so used to going my regular way.

Nevertheless, I turned off and drove another way to work. Later that day, I learned there was an accident on my usual route to work around the same time I would have been driving that way. Thank you, Lord, for helping me to be more sensitive to the Holy Spirit.

July 11, 2011 — Where to Place My Faith

Have you ever had so many things going on in your life and needed so many answers that you're not sure where to put your faith? How about placing your faith in thanksgiving? Thank you, Lord, that even in my times of uncertainty, you will speak a new word.

Thank you for the comfort and peace of your word. Thank you for the Holy Spirit, who is my comforter and teacher. Thank you for protecting Lexi and me and for always making a way for us. Love you, Lord!

Lord, thank you for showing me where to place my faith, and that is in you. Thank you, Jesus.

July 16, 2011 — Nothing Broken or Bruised

Coming into the main door of my building, somehow, my heel got caught under it. I haven't felt physical pain like that in a long time! But thanks to God, nothing was broken, and surprisingly, I didn't even have a bruise. Thank you, Lord!

July 18, 2011 — An On-time God

I parked my car in a place I shouldn't have. When I was parking, I didn't notice the sign that said, "Cars will be towed." Hours later, when I got back to my car, another car was towed! Thank you, Lord, that I came back right in time!

Moments of Gratitude

July 19, 2011 — $108.68

A few months ago, I got a traffic ticket that I forgot about. Today, I received a notice in the mail saying that I needed to immediately pay the $108.68 ticket. Or my driving privileges would be affected.

I checked my account, and would you believe that I had precisely $108.68? Can you say, "Praise Dance?" Thank you, Lord!

October 11, 2011 — Get Up and Get Out

Father, thank you for another birthday! I am so grateful. I was lying on my bed admiring my new book, *Praying for Our Children*. It took me about five years to complete it, though I had been praying the prayers over Lexi for years. I had worked extra hard to get it done in time for my birthday.

Suddenly, it occurred to me that I was 34 years old and still not married. Neither did I have any prospects in sight. And since I had stopped going out with guys that I knew were not the ones, I hadn't had a date in forever.

Holy Spirit said, *"get up and get out."* I was shocked. So I jumped up, got on my computer, and searched for activities in and around my community. I remembered the event First Friday, which was an event held monthly in various cities in North Jersey. So I scheduled First Friday on my calendar for November 4th, 2011. Thank you, Lord.

November 4, 2011 — Promoting My Book

Abba, The last few months have been extremely busy with me finalizing my book, *Praying for Our Children*. I had to do a lot of rewriting, finding editors and publishers, and all that goes with publishing a book. It is finally finished, and I am going to the First Friday networking event to market my book and connect with other entrepreneurs. Father, thank you for your favor.

November 5, 2011

Good morning, father. It's about 5:30 am, and I am up early thanking you for last night. I stepped out on faith to market my book and put myself out there a the First Friday Networking event.

I met a lovely gentleman that I would love to talk to again. He seems nice, well-spoken, saved, has a great job, has never been married, and has no kids. But he wants to be married and have children. We exchanged numbers, and he said he would call me to take me out.

Lawd, I'm excited to see if he is the one. He is so handsome, and you know I love a handsome man. Now, I'm just going to continue to put myself out there more and hope that my path will cross with my Boaz. Thank you, Lord.

November 6, 2011 — New Journal

Lawd, I need to buy a new journal; this one is almost full.

September 29, 2012 — I Didn't Forget

My car is in the shop for about a week. Sitting on the bus, upset as I could be, the Lord said: *"Satan attached himself to your car. You must get on the bus. You are upset, but don't get upset. Praise me that you didn't forget how to take a bus!"*

Sometimes, we find ourselves in unfavorable positions. It's natural to get upset, but instead of getting upset, praise God amid it! I am thankful that I didn't forget how to take the bus.

I did not forget waking up earlier than most to leave the house by 7 a.m. to drop Lexi off at school. Then get back on the bus to get to my classes or work-study assignment by 8:30. Thank you, Lord, that I didn't forget how to get on the bus. Thank you, Lord!

October 11-12, 2012 — Will Your Marry Me?

I have another journal about my dating journey coming soon, but I just wanted to mention here that on my birthday, that wonderful man I met proposed to me. And guess what I said? "YES!!"

January 7, 2013 — A Moment in Time

Early Saturday morning, the temperature is exceptionally lovely and unseasonably warm for this time of year. Lying in bed thinking that this is the MOMENT, the time in my life that I can honestly say is the happiest I have been in a long time. Then I began to think back on memories of other times when I was happy. When was I carefree and laughed like there was no tomorrow? When was the last time someone cared for me that made a difference in my life?

Closing my eyes, I begin to flip back through the pages of my life. Walking down the hallway of my life, the corridors of time, and I think again, a moment in time, as a little girl, running, playing, and laughing. I was in a dress I'm sure my grandmother made from materials she bought at the marketplace.

I was happy and carefree in my first home in Clarendon, Jamaica. The worries and concerns of this world were nowhere in my mind. It was *a moment in time.*

And so, I lay here thinking of the more recent events in my life. The joy of publishing my first book, *Praying for Our Children*. Parents being blessed with it and the pleasure and blessing of seeing Alexia growing and flourishing. I thank you, Lord.

You see, when you've been discouraged in prayer, you must make yourself pray! Make yourself believe again, bend your will, faith, and emotions to trust and believe in God again. Thank you, Lord.

May 11, 2013 — This Is My Season

Father, today is the day that I have prayed, fasted, cried, and waited for. For as long as I can remember, I have always wanted to be married and have a father figure for my beautiful Lexi. Father, Michael, and I courtship were so beautiful. He proposed in less than a year, and we are getting married just a few months later. Lord, I thank you so much.

May 11, 2013, a beautiful sunny and rainy day, I walked down the aisle to *"This Is My Season"* by Donald Lawrence and married the man I have been praying for. Today we said, "I do to each other and forever." Thank You, Lord. I just love my Mr. Wonderful.

May 31, 2013 — Flash Back

It's 5:30 a.m., and I am up doing my devotional, reading out of one of my books. This devotional has color pages with some of the most beautiful pictures I've ever seen. As I flip through, the Lord reminded me of the little garden I had when I was about eight to ten years old. I started it with one plant from my neighbor, Ms. Doris, and then another. The little garden that began with one flower turned out to be one of the most beautiful gardens you have ever seen in no time.

One day, as I came home from school, I saw a cement truck in our driveway. My heart sank. My books carelessly fell as I ran to where my garden was. The tears began to well up in my eyes as I saw the cement in the place where my beautiful garden had been.

You see, my parents were beginning to do repairs and expansions on our house. While we had an extremely long driveway, we didn't have much space outside the driveway. Our driveway was also connected to our tank, and since we didn't use that part of the driveway often, that spot was perfect for my beautiful flower garden.

As I stood there, tears rolled down my little face as I thought about all the hard work, love, and attention I had given to my beautiful garden. Why couldn't they find another spot to put the cement, I thought. As I stood there crying, I felt that I would never plant another garden.

Strangely, I remember that incident almost thirty years later. Also, I find it ironic that I have not kept any plants over the years. As I think back, I believe that my unconscious mind remembered my beautiful garden that was destroyed.

The Lord has now blessed us with a beautiful home with a lot of land, even though we are waiting to close. With this new revelation, I believe it's time for me to plant another garden. This time, I don't have to worry about someone pouring cement on it or destroying it. I believe I will get a landscaper to help me bring my childhood dream to reality.

July 18, 2013 — Welcome Home

Another mention here is that my wonderful husband Michael, me, and my daughter closed on our beautiful four-bedroom, 2.5 bathrooms, and three floors house. It took us seven months, but finally, we have a home. Thank You, Lord.

May 11, 2014 — Congratulations

Today my husband and I celebrated our first anniversary, and we are one month pregnant. Thank You, Lord.

January 4, 2015 — Children are Gifts

Thank you, Lord, that today at 2:18 pm, you blessed us with a healthy, beautiful baby boy weighing 7 lbs and 7 ounces. Michael Thompson Jr is so precious. Thank You, father.

May 2016 — More than Sevenfold Blessing

Remember earlier when I mentioned the garden I had when I was a little girl that was destroyed? I also shared that I never kept any plants or flowers other than those I received as gifts that would last about a week over the years.

Well, flip this book over and look at the cover's flowers. Yes! The beautiful flowers on the cover of this book are flowers from my garden. There was a giant rosebush at the back door when we bought our house. It was so tall that it covered most of my kitchen window.

I did get a landscaper who planted some other beautiful flowers for the season. Aren't they beautiful? For the past three years, I have brought my co-workers and friends roses from the beautiful bush by my back door.

I tell you, God restores. He promised that He would bless us sevenfold. Thank you, Lord.

July 21, 2016 — Won't He Do It?

Today, I parked my truck in the parking lot and walked towards the office. I was about halfway through the parking lot when I felt the need to go back and check to see if I had locked the door.

The door needs to stay unlocked for the attendants to move it, if necessary. At first, I hesitated because I wouldn't think I locked my keys in the truck.

Finally, I decided to go back and check the door. It was open, but the ID that I needed to enter my office building was on the ground by the truck.

This example is one reason we need to be sensitive to the Holy Spirit's leading. Thank you, Lord!

2016 — *God Will Always Make a Way*

This year has been full of anxiety, change, and new beginnings for Alexia and me. She has graduated, and it's time for her to move on from the school she's been attending for thirteen years. A school where all her friends, favorite teachers, and aides are. It's time to move on from her haven into this big world.

Leading up to graduation, Alexia would often say, "Mommy, I don't want to leave my school. I'm going to miss my friends and my teachers." With pain and sometimes uncertainty, I would let her know that it would be okay and that it was time for her to move on, meet new people, and make new friends. I told her that it would be an adventure for her to look forward to.

Alexia's prom was huge! She found a dress that she fell in love with. She got a perm, nails done, makeup done, and my baby looked like a supermodel. She even got a limo, and she danced the night away with her friends.

Then it was graduation, and my baby looked like the scholar she is. And then there was no more school. All this year, I've been trying to find a program for her myself, instead of waiting for the state, which takes forever. I found quite a few that I liked, but some didn't call back, while others said they were already full. Yet others, in my estimation, wouldn't accept her because she didn't look like their ethnicity and had no plans of "integrating."

Additionally, transitioning from high school to a day program has gotten too tedious in the last few years. And the way day programs are paid for has also changed. Before, a young adult with special needs could graduate this week and be in a day program next week. Not so anymore. Some students are still home a whole year later, waiting to be placed.

Therefore, I started to look around and do the necessary paperwork a long time before Lexi graduated since her heart's desire is to attend college. However, as a special needs student, there aren't any colleges that can meet her needs. A few colleges accept special needs students; however, Alexia cannot navigate campuses independently. Also, special needs students would have to be tested to get into the colleges.

Unfortunately, Alexia is not able to test to get in. It took me a few years, but I did my research with her and attended transitional events to find something for her. Finally, I think she understands no college can meet her needs at this time. We have been transitioning to a day program and vocational training instead.

One day after graduation, Alexia and I were home, and she came to me and said that she was ready to go to a day program, meet new people, make new friends, and have new adventures. I felt as if my heart dropped. I grabbed her hand and told her to come and kneel so that we could pray.

While praying, the phone rang, and it was a day program that I forgot I had called. The lady stated that she had returned my call and left a message, but I didn't return her call. I was shocked because I didn't get any messages about that day program.

Saints! One day, I did everything we needed to get her into the program. The state would take months to give her a budget, so that meant I had to pay out of my pocket. Thank God. He had a ram in the bush to offset some of the cost. Instead of paying the regular state fee, I was given a discounted rate of $90 per day. Yes, you read that correctly.

I arranged for Lexi to attend two days per week until her state budget came through.

One day, Alexia texted me and said she wanted to go another day each week, and once again, my heartfelt as if it broke into a million pieces. I really couldn't afford for her to attend another day. So, I called the program, and would you believe that the director was there? I asked if anything could be done with the price so that Lexi could attend the third day. I explained that I have been paying. I haven't missed any payments. Lexi liked the program, and she would like to attend three days per week instead of two days, but I could not afford to pay for the third day.

The Lord showed us favor, and she was able to attend three days a week at a reduced price, and the additional fee that I had to pay was only $20! Saints, when I tell you that God has been good to Alexia and me, He has been good. God has always made a way for Alexia. From the time she was in my sixteen-year-old womb until today, God has always made a way for her! And those are the memories I continue to hold on to. Those are the benefits I continue to rehearse in my mind, according to **Psalm 103**. Amen!

In June 2018, Alexia had an incident at her program, and I pulled her out and contacted the state and our Support Coordinator. Thankfully, after about two weeks, I was able to get her into another program, along with another program for community activity. Now she is attending two day programs that can meet her needs and give her the community inclusion she needs. Everything has been great, and I am so thankful to the Lord. Thank you, Jesus, for always making a way for my baby girl.

2020 — *Lexi Update*

At the publication of *Moments of Gratitude*, Alexia is still attending both of her day programs. Her state budget came through in September 2016. Unfortunately, because Alexia is "high functioning," her yearly budget is only $22,000 per year. However, $22K per year is not enough to attend a program every day. An additional thirty-five days for her calendar year is needed. So we budget her days around the program's closure or staff development with holidays. Also, if Alexia needs to be absent, those days are subtracted.

Saints, I am still thankful for what the Lord has done. Daily, I pray for the Lord to continue to bless and make a way for Lexi's budget to increase. I am so grateful for the goodness of the Lord, and I continue to pray for the manifestation of the Lord's total healing for Alexia.

Furthermore, I continue to pray for every parent who has a child with special needs. No one understands what special needs parents go through because it's as if we have a forever baby for most of us. My prayer is that the Lord will bless and keep us and give us grace.

I pray daily for God to manifest his healing power in Alexia's life and all special needs children. I pray for my future children and my bloodline for the power and blood of Jesus Christ to annihilate all attacks and generational curses and sickness in Jesus' name.

Thank you, Lord, and I call it done in Jesus' name. Amen.

Janice Hylton Thompson

Testimony Time and New Dating Journal

While I mentioned a few times, I could not end this book without sharing a sneak peek of my testimony of how my husband and I met and got married. I have a whole other journal on my dating devotionals, but I wanted to share my blessing here with you in detail.

Throughout this book, I prayed, confessed, and believed God for my husband. And I want to encourage you that if you are believing God for your husband or a miracle, please keep on believing and confessing God's word because, in due time, the promise will come. Though ladies, I think we must do our part in making ourselves available to meet our Boaz.

Remember all those prayers I prayed for my husband? Let me tell you what the Lord did for me. I had decided that I needed to focus on my book, teaching, and other writing projects. Plus, I wasn't meeting the type of man I wanted to marry. Therefore, I wasn't dating, aka gathering data, on guys. My life had returned to work, church, life with Lexi, and hours of writing and reading.

I completed my first book, *Praying for Our Children*, which took me about five years. I celebrated my 34th birthday on October 11, 2011. Laying on my bed, suddenly, I realized that I still was not married. But neither was I meeting anyone I would share a meal with, much less marry.

Furthermore, I realized that I wasn't meeting anyone because I wasn't going out to meet anyone. While lying on the bed, it's as if the Spirit of the Lord spoke to me and said, *"Get Up and Go Out."* Lol.

I remember jumping up out of bed, going online to search for events in my area; plays, movies, etc. I remembered a monthly event called "First Fridays." It's a networking event in New Jersey that meets every month in a local city. So I scheduled that on my calendar for November 4th.

To get out there more, I went to a few restaurants alone, sat at a bar, and watched the game. I attended events in my community and various churches. Every chance I got to market my book, I took it. I attended a few plays and some wine tastings, and a few other activities.

I asked my co-worker if she wanted to attend the First Friday Event with me, and she agreed. I also asked two other church sisters because they were single and needed to get out of the house and church, but they declined. Well, I got dressed up, got my hair and nails done, put on a gracious smile and attitude, and attended First Friday with my books in hand and a prayer that I would meet my husband.

I got to the event, and my co-worker and I were sitting across from each other. Then came the sheriff officer's wife at our job, whom we knew. We talked and laughed. After a while, in came an extraordinarily handsome and impeccably dress gentleman.

It so happened that he knew the wife of the sheriff officer because they attended the same high school together. The gentleman sat beside me and introduced himself as Michael Thompson. We all talked and exchanged contact info, and so on. Remember, this is a networking event, so exchanging contact info was necessary.

Later, my friend motioned to me and texted me that she thought Michael liked me. I text back, "no, I think he likes you because he's talking to you a lot." She then texts back that no, she believes he liked me because every time I got up and worked the room, he followed me with his eyes until I came back to my seat.

Michael offered to get us something to drink, but we declined because we didn't know this strange man. Lol. After we talked more about jobs and families. Michael asked about my writing and books. And then he complimented me and said, "You must have your mother's legs." Ladies, he got my attention! I smiled, gave him more legs, turned my whole self around to face him, and gave him a whole lot of smile and sexiness.

And that's how it all began. We talked the evening away. I learned that Michael has never been married or had kids. But he wanted to get married and have kids. He gave me his business card, and his title was Executive Vice President. And do you want to guess where he worked? Remember what I prayed?

Oh, there's just so much to, and the lessons I learned. I will share in an upcoming book of my Dating Devotionals, where I talked to the Lord about the guys I was dating.

So be sure to be on the lookout, and thank you so much.

Final Words

I pray that you were encouraged and blessed by this book: *Moments of Gratitude*. I pray that the stories included and my moments of gratitude blessed and encouraged you to go on in God. I hope you feel better and will begin to thank your way out of your valley of discouragement. Thanksgiving works because it requires you to open your mouth and give God thanks regardless of your circumstances.

One of the things I love about my *Moments of Gratitude* is that I could see the growth in myself, my faith, and my walk with Christ. As you journal your faith, I pray that you will see the growth in yourself also.

Remember, there is always something to thank God for! You just must look for it. Be blessed and encouraged in the Lord, and I will continue to pray for you as I ask that you continue to pray for the Body of Christ and me.

Janice
Thank You

Few of my Go-to and Favorite Psalms

I absolutely love the book of Psalm. Psalm is my go-to book for comfort, and I wanted to share a few of my favorite Psalms with you. I have a book coming soon on Psalm. I cannot wait for you to read it.

Psalm 1

¹ Blessed is the man that walketh not in the counsel of the ungodly, nor standeth in the way of sinners, nor sitteth in the seat of the scornful.

² But his delight is in the law of the Lord; and in his law doth he meditate day and night.

³ And he shall be like a tree planted by the rivers of water, that bringeth forth his fruit in his season; his leaf also shall not wither; and whatsoever he doeth shall prosper.

⁴ The ungodly are not so: but are like the chaff which the wind driveth away.

⁵ Therefore the ungodly shall not stand in the judgment, nor sinners in the congregation of the righteous.

⁶ For the Lord knoweth the way of the righteous: but the way of the ungodly shall perish.

Psalm 17

¹ Hear the right, O Lord, attend unto my cry, give ear unto my prayer, that goeth not out of feigned lips.

² Let my sentence come forth from thy presence; let thine eyes behold the things that are equal.

³ Thou hast proved mine heart; thou hast visited me in the night; thou hast tried me, and shalt find nothing; I am purposed that my mouth shall not transgress.

⁴ Concerning the works of men, by the word of thy lips I have kept me from the paths of the destroyer.

⁵ Hold up my goings in thy paths, that my footsteps slip not.

⁶ I have called upon thee, for thou wilt hear me, O God: incline thine ear unto me, and hear my speech.

⁷ Shew thy marvellous lovingkindness, O thou that savest by thy right hand them which put their trust in thee from those that rise up against them.

⁸ Keep me as the apple of the eye, hide me under the shadow of thy wings,

⁹ From the wicked that oppress me, from my deadly enemies, who compass me about.

¹⁰ They are inclosed in their own fat: with their mouth they speak proudly.

¹¹ They have now compassed us in our steps: they have set their eyes bowing down to the earth;

¹² Like as a lion that is greedy of his prey, and as it were a young lion lurking in secret places.

¹³ Arise, O Lord, disappoint him, cast him down: deliver my soul from the wicked, which is thy sword:

¹⁴ From men which are thy hand, O Lord, from men of the world, which have their portion in this life, and whose belly thou fillest with thy hid treasure: they are full of children, and leave the rest of their substance to their babes.

¹⁵ As for me, I will behold thy face in righteousness: I shall be satisfied, when I awake, with thy likeness.

Psalm 18

¹ I will love thee, O Lord, my strength.

² The Lord is my rock, and my fortress, and my deliverer; my God, my strength, in whom I will trust; my buckler, and the horn of my salvation, and my high tower.

³ I will call upon the Lord, who is worthy to be praised: so shall I be saved from mine enemies.

⁴ The sorrows of death compassed me, and the floods of ungodly men made me afraid.

⁵ The sorrows of hell compassed me about: the snares of death prevented me.

⁶ In my distress I called upon the Lord, and cried unto my God: he heard my voice out of his temple, and my cry came before him, even into his ears.

⁷ Then the earth shook and trembled; the foundations also of the hills moved and were shaken, because he was wroth.

⁸ There went up a smoke out of his nostrils, and fire out of his mouth devoured: coals were kindled by it.

⁹ He bowed the heavens also, and came down: and darkness was under his feet.

¹⁰ And he rode upon a cherub, and did fly: yea, he did fly upon the wings of the wind.

¹¹ He made darkness his secret place; his pavilion round about him were dark waters and thick clouds of the skies.

¹² At the brightness that was before him his thick clouds passed, hail stones and coals of fire.

¹³ The Lord also thundered in the heavens, and the Highest gave his voice; hail stones and coals of fire.

¹⁴ Yea, he sent out his arrows, and scattered them; and he shot out lightnings, and discomfited them.

¹⁵ Then the channels of waters were seen, and the foundations of the world were discovered at thy rebuke, O Lord, at the blast of the breath of thy nostrils.

¹⁶ He sent from above, he took me, he drew me out of many waters.

¹⁷ He delivered me from my strong enemy, and from them which hated me: for they were too strong for me.

¹⁸ They prevented me in the day of my calamity: but the Lord was my stay.

¹⁹ He brought me forth also into a large place; he delivered me, because he delighted in me.

Moments of Gratitude

[20] The Lord rewarded me according to my righteousness; according to the cleanness of my hands hath he recompensed me.

[21] For I have kept the ways of the Lord, and have not wickedly departed from my God.

[22] For all his judgments were before me, and I did not put away his statutes from me.

[23] I was also upright before him, and I kept myself from mine iniquity.

[24] Therefore hath the Lord recompensed me according to my righteousness, according to the cleanness of my hands in his eyesight.

[25] With the merciful thou wilt shew thyself merciful; with an upright man thou wilt shew thyself upright;

[26] With the pure thou wilt shew thyself pure; and with the froward thou wilt shew thyself froward.

[27] For thou wilt save the afflicted people; but wilt bring down high looks.

[28] For thou wilt light my candle: the Lord my God will enlighten my darkness.

[29] For by thee I have run through a troop; and by my God have I leaped over a wall.

³⁰ As for God, his way is perfect: the word of the Lord is tried: he is a buckler to all those that trust in him.

³¹ For who is God save the Lord? or who is a rock save our God?

³² It is God that girdeth me with strength, and maketh my way perfect.

³³ He maketh my feet like hinds' feet, and setteth me upon my high places.

³⁴ He teacheth my hands to war, so that a bow of steel is broken by mine arms.

³⁵ Thou hast also given me the shield of thy salvation: and thy right hand hath holden me up, and thy gentleness hath made me great.

³⁶ Thou hast enlarged my steps under me, that my feet did not slip.

³⁷ I have pursued mine enemies, and overtaken them: neither did I turn again till they were consumed.

³⁸ I have wounded them that they were not able to rise: they are fallen under my feet.

³⁹ For thou hast girded me with strength unto the battle: thou hast subdued under me those that rose up against me.

⁴⁰ Thou hast also given me the necks of mine enemies; that I might destroy them that hate me.

⁴¹ They cried, but there was none to save them: even unto the Lord, but he answered them not.

⁴² Then did I beat them small as the dust before the wind: I did cast them out as the dirt in the streets.

⁴³ Thou hast delivered me from the strivings of the people; and thou hast made me the head of the heathen: a people whom I have not known shall serve me.

⁴⁴ As soon as they hear of me, they shall obey me: the strangers shall submit themselves unto me.

⁴⁵ The strangers shall fade away, and be afraid out of their close places.

⁴⁶ The Lord liveth; and blessed be my rock; and let the God of my salvation be exalted.

⁴⁷ It is God that avengeth me, and subdueth the people under me.

⁴⁸ He delivereth me from mine enemies: yea, thou liftest me up above those that rise up against me: thou hast delivered me from the violent man.

⁴⁹ Therefore will I give thanks unto thee, O Lord, among the heathen, and sing praises unto thy name.

⁵⁰ Great deliverance giveth he to his king; and sheweth mercy to his anointed, to David, and to his seed for evermore.

Psalm 23

¹ The Lord is my shepherd; I shall not want.

² He maketh me to lie down in green pastures: he leadeth me beside the still waters.

³ He restoreth my soul: he leadeth me in the paths of righteousness for his name's sake.

⁴ Yea, though I walk through the valley of the shadow of death, I will fear no evil: for thou art with me; thy rod and thy staff they comfort me.

⁵ Thou preparest a table before me in the presence of mine enemies: thou anointest my head with oil; my cup runneth over.

⁶ Surely goodness and mercy shall follow me all the days of my life: and I will dwell in the house of the Lord for ever.

Psalm 27

¹ The Lord is my light and my salvation; whom shall I fear? the Lord is the strength of my life; of whom shall I be afraid?

² When the wicked, even mine enemies and my foes, came upon me to eat up my flesh, they stumbled and fell.

³ Though an host should encamp against me, my heart shall not fear: though war should rise against me, in this will I be confident.

⁴ One thing have I desired of the Lord, that will I seek after; that I may dwell in the house of the Lord all the days of my life, to behold the beauty of the Lord, and to enquire in his temple.

⁵ For in the time of trouble he shall hide me in his pavilion: in the secret of his tabernacle shall he hide me; he shall set me up upon a rock.

⁶ And now shall mine head be lifted up above mine enemies round about me: therefore will I offer in his tabernacle sacrifices of joy; I will sing, yea, I will sing praises unto the Lord.

⁷ Hear, O Lord, when I cry with my voice: have mercy also upon me, and answer me.

⁸ When thou saidst, Seek ye my face; my heart said unto thee, Thy face, Lord, will I seek.

⁹ Hide not thy face far from me; put not thy servant away in anger: thou hast been my help; leave me not, neither forsake me, O God of my salvation.

¹⁰ When my father and my mother forsake me, then the Lord will take me up.

¹¹ Teach me thy way, O Lord, and lead me in a plain path, because of mine enemies.

¹² Deliver me not over unto the will of mine enemies: for false witnesses are risen up against me, and such as breathe out cruelty.

¹³ I had fainted, unless I had believed to see the goodness of the Lord in the land of the living.

¹⁴ Wait on the Lord: be of good courage, and he shall strengthen thine heart: wait, I say, on the Lord.

Psalm 91

¹ He that dwelleth in the secret place of the most High shall abide under the shadow of the Almighty.

² I will say of the Lord, He is my refuge and my fortress: my God; in him will I trust.

³ Surely he shall deliver thee from the snare of the fowler, and from the noisome pestilence.

⁴ He shall cover thee with his feathers, and under his wings shalt thou trust: his truth shall be thy shield and buckler.

⁵ Thou shalt not be afraid for the terror by night; nor for the arrow that flieth by day;

⁶ Nor for the pestilence that walketh in darkness; nor for the destruction that wasteth at noonday.

⁷ A thousand shall fall at thy side, and ten thousand at thy right hand; but it shall not come nigh thee.

⁸ Only with thine eyes shalt thou behold and see the reward of the wicked.

⁹ Because thou hast made the Lord, which is my refuge, even the most High, thy habitation;

¹⁰ There shall no evil befall thee, neither shall any plague come nigh thy dwelling.

¹¹ For he shall give his angels charge over thee, to keep thee in all thy ways.

¹² They shall bear thee up in their hands, lest thou dash thy foot against a stone.

¹³ Thou shalt tread upon the lion and adder: the young lion and the dragon shalt thou trample under feet.

¹⁴ Because he hath set his love upon me, therefore will I deliver him: I will set him on high, because he hath known my name.

¹⁵ He shall call upon me, and I will answer him: I will be with him in trouble; I will deliver him, and honour him.

¹⁶ With long life will I satisfy him, and shew him my salvation.

Psalm 100

¹ Make a joyful noise unto the Lord, all ye lands.

² Serve the Lord with gladness: come before his presence with singing.

³ Know ye that the Lord he is God: it is he that hath made us, and not we ourselves; we are his people, and the sheep of his pasture.

⁴ Enter into his gates with thanksgiving, and into his courts with praise: be thankful unto him, and bless his name.

⁵ For the Lord is good; his mercy is everlasting; and his truth endureth to all generations.

Janice Hylton Thompson

Psalm 103

¹ Bless the Lord, O my soul: and all that is within me, bless his holy name.

² Bless the Lord, O my soul, and forget not all his benefits:

³ Who forgiveth all thine iniquities; who healeth all thy diseases;

⁴ Who redeemeth thy life from destruction; who crowneth thee with lovingkindness and tender mercies;

⁵ Who satisfieth thy mouth with good things; so that thy youth is renewed like the eagle's.

⁶ The Lord executeth righteousness and judgment for all that are oppressed.

⁷ He made known his ways unto Moses, his acts unto the children of Israel.

⁸ The Lord is merciful and gracious, slow to anger, and plenteous in mercy.

⁹ He will not always chide: neither will he keep his anger for ever.

¹⁰ He hath not dealt with us after our sins; nor rewarded us according to our iniquities.

¹¹ For as the heaven is high above the earth, so great is his mercy toward them that fear him.

¹² As far as the east is from the west, so far hath he removed our transgressions from us.

¹³ Like as a father pitieth his children, so the Lord pitieth them that fear him.

¹⁴ For he knoweth our frame; he remembereth that we are dust.

¹⁵ As for man, his days are as grass: as a flower of the field, so he flourisheth.

¹⁶ For the wind passeth over it, and it is gone; and the place thereof shall know it no more.

¹⁷ But the mercy of the Lord is from everlasting to everlasting upon them that fear him, and his righteousness unto children's children;

¹⁸ To such as keep his covenant, and to those that remember his commandments to do them.

¹⁹ The Lord hath prepared his throne in the heavens; and his kingdom ruleth over all.

²⁰ Bless the Lord, ye his angels, that excel in strength, that do his commandments, hearkening unto the voice of his word.

[21] Bless ye the Lord, all ye his hosts; ye ministers of his, that do his pleasure.

[22] Bless the Lord, all his works in all places of his dominion: bless the Lord, O my soul.

About the Author

Janice is wife to her wonderful husband, Michael Sr., and mom of two children born 20 years apart. Janice's beautiful and fashionable daughter, Alexia, and her most handsome, curious, and joyful son, Michael Jr.

Janice loves to read and write; she writes passionately about subjects that mean the most to her. Additionally, Janice loves to tackle those "rock the boat" subjects.

Janice loves to spend time with her family, making their favorite meals, watching movies, enjoying a day at the park, shopping and doing girls' stuff with Alexia, and playing and learning with Michael Jr.

Janice's motto is "Teaching & Writing in Simplicity That Even A Child Will Understand." Janice's teaching ministry is under the covering of her spiritual father, Bishop Marvin Bradshaw Sr.

Janice is the author of several books and has been writing for over 20 years. Her published books include:

1. Praying for Our Children
2. In Christ I Am
3. In Christ, I Am Prayer Journal
4. In Christ, I Am Bible Study Journal
5. The Phenomenon of Donald J Trump - The GOP Nominee
6. The Naked Wife
7. 23 Types of Guys You Might Meet
8. Moments of Gratitude
9. Moments of Gratitude Thank You Journal
10. 31 Days to Not Being a Girlfriend if You Want to Be a Wife - Printable

Janice Hylton Blog @ www.janicehyltonblog.com encourages and empowers women to walk in their royalty anointing as The King's Daughters.

If you would like to connect with Janice, you can do so on Facebook:
1. Author Janice Hylton-Thompson
2. Janice Hylton Blog
3. Praying for Our Children

You can also connect with Janice on YouTube @Janice Hylton.

www.ingramcontent.com/pod-product-compliance
Lightning Source LLC
Chambersburg PA
CBHW031351040426
42444CB00005B/252